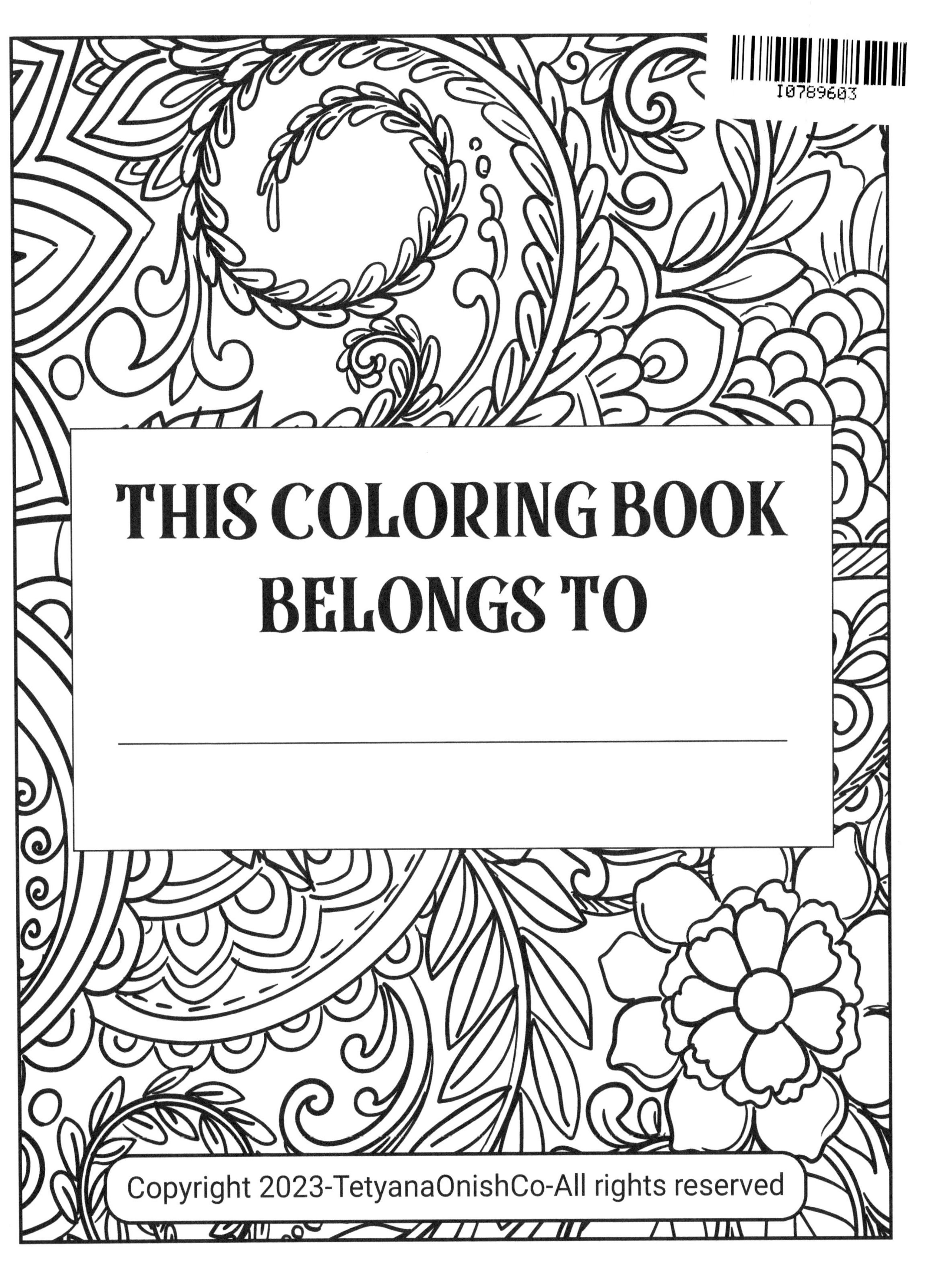

THIS COLORING BOOK BELONGS TO

____

COLOR TEST PAGE

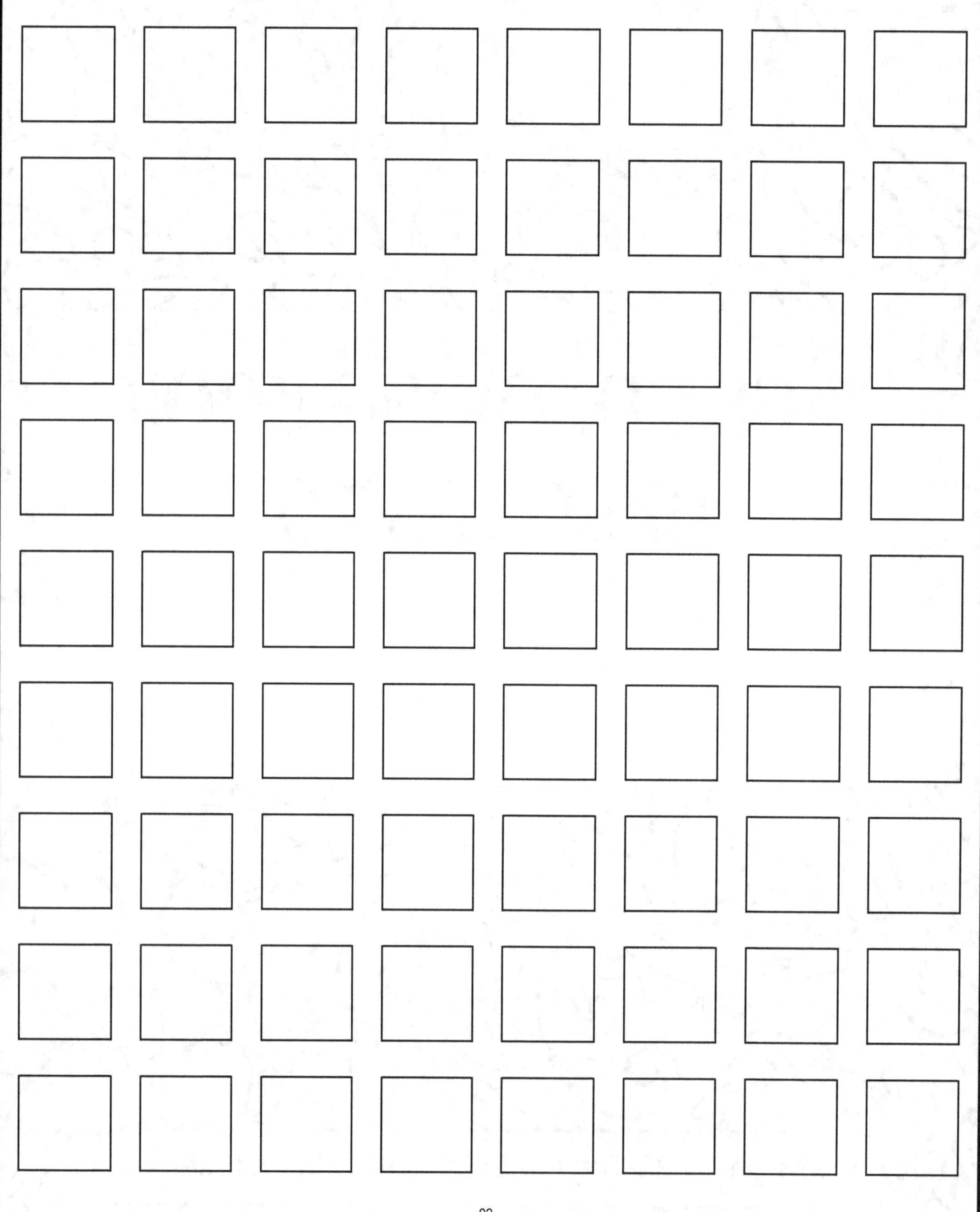

INSTRUCTION

Do these before each coloring session:

1. Take a deep breath and relax.

2. Color today's page. Pay attention to your feelings and emotions. Write them down and notice how they change through the process.

3. Observe which color pencils or markers your hand (subconscious mind) picks. Write down the chosen color(s) and reflect on its significance to you.

4. Unfold your inner story as insights emerge. Write it down.

5. Replace old (negative) memories with the beautiful picture you just created. Consider it a new program for your subconscious mind to follow and fulfill. Write it down.

6. Finish by expressing gratitude to your subconscious mind for its excellent work and collaboration in crafting a more radiant and promising future from this moment onward.

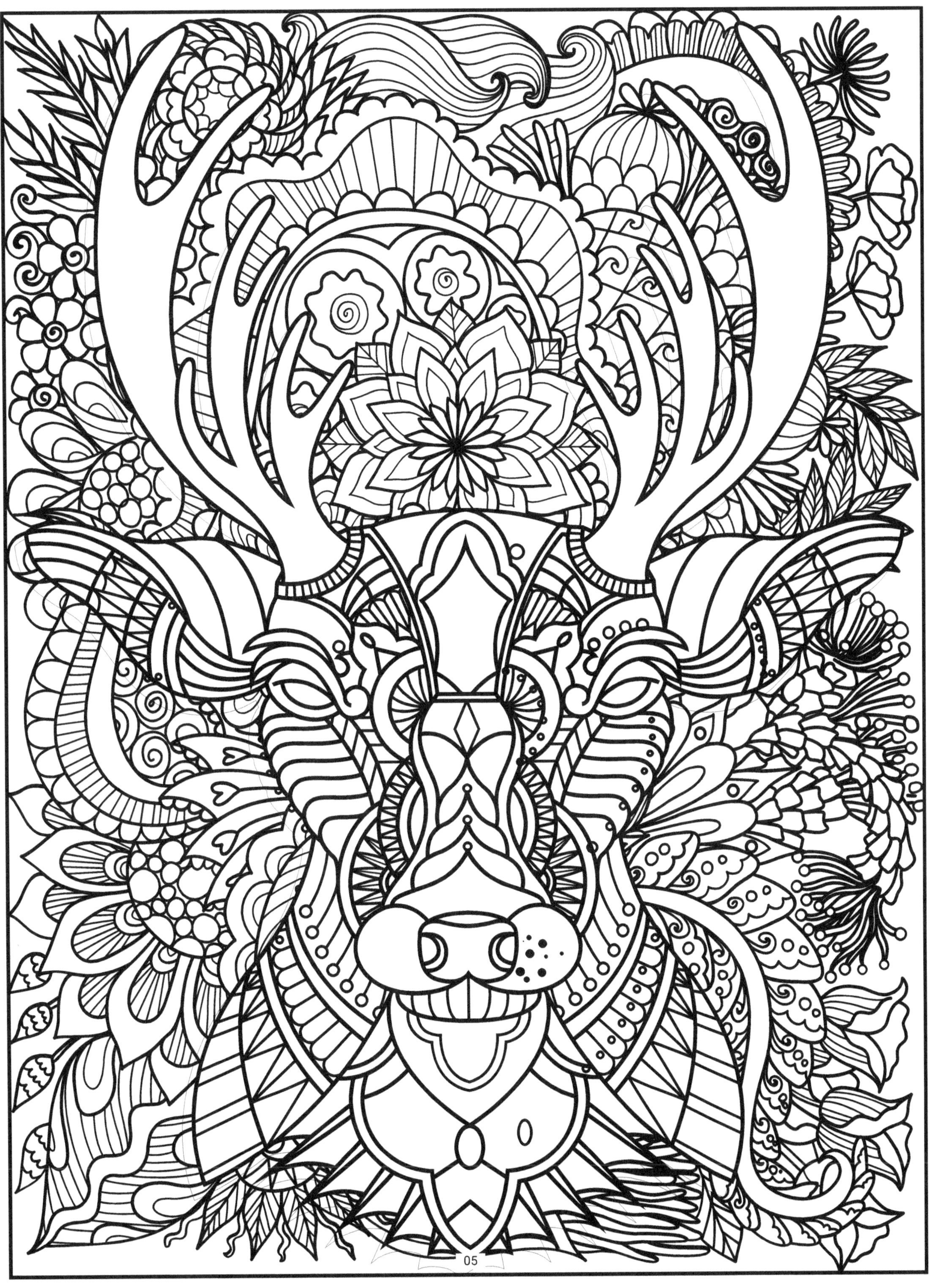

What Emotions Are Emerging as You Color?

What Symbolism or Significance Do You Attribute to the Colors You've Chose?

Can You Describe the Story or Narrative Behind Your Colorful Picture?

What new things come up from the old memories and experiences?

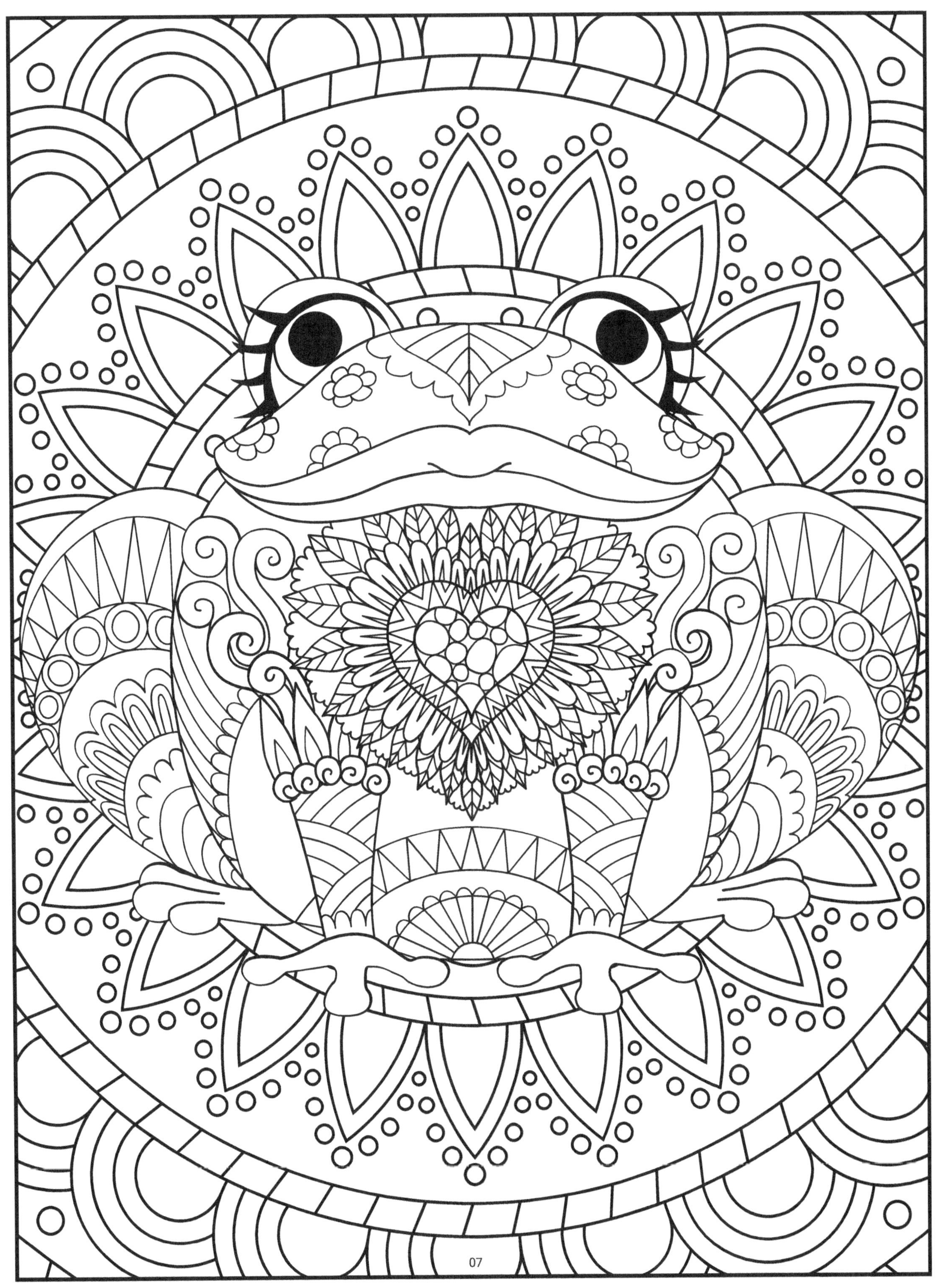

What Emotions Are Emerging as You Color?

What Symbolism or Significance Do You Attribute to the Colors You've Chose?

Can You Describe the Story or Narrative Behind Your Colorful Picture?

What new things come up from the old memories and experiences?

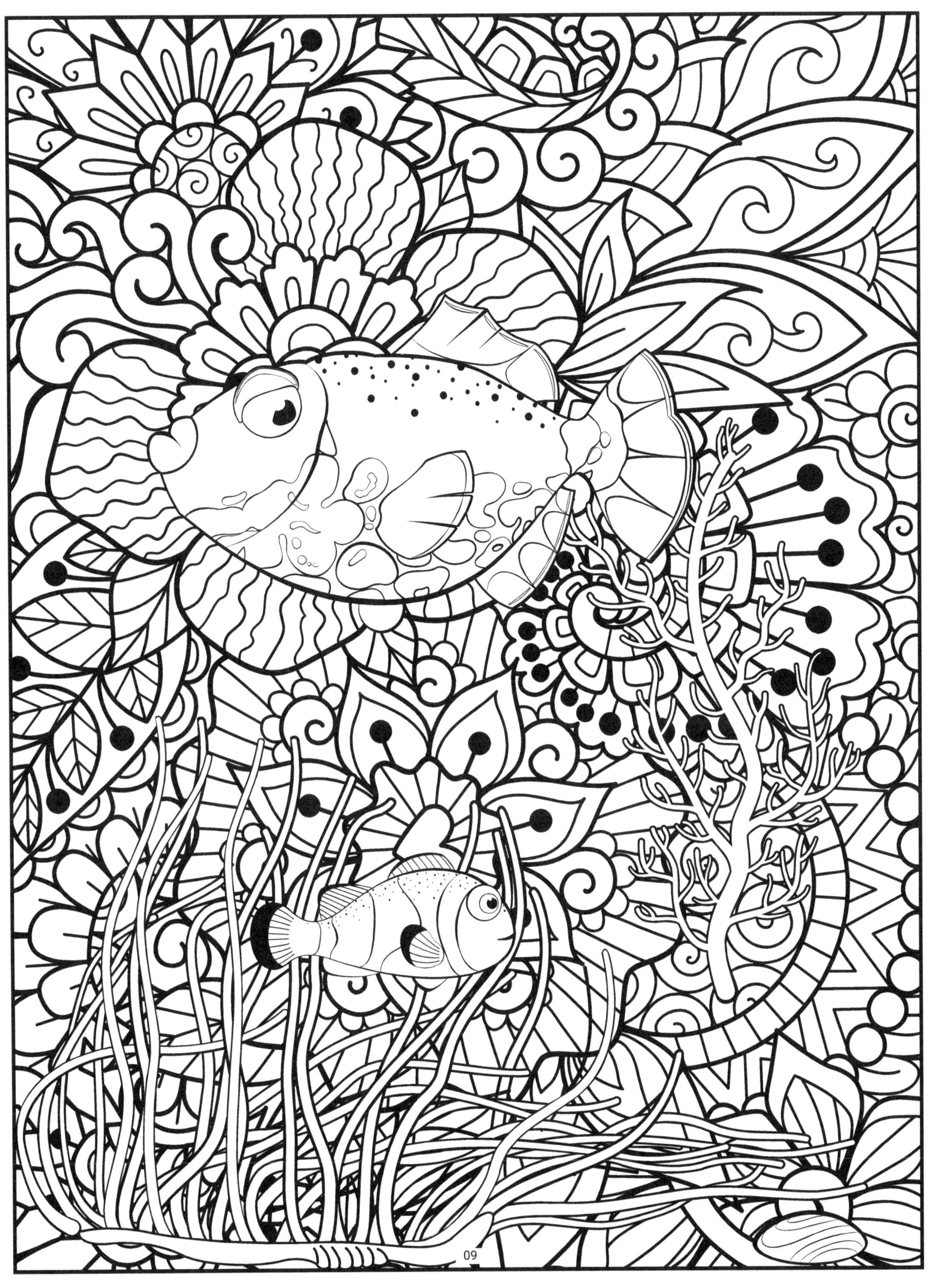

What Emotions Are Emerging as You Color?

What Symbolism or Significance Do You Attribute to the Colors You've Chose?

Can You Describe the Story or Narrative Behind Your Colorful Picture?

What new things come up from the old memories and experiences?

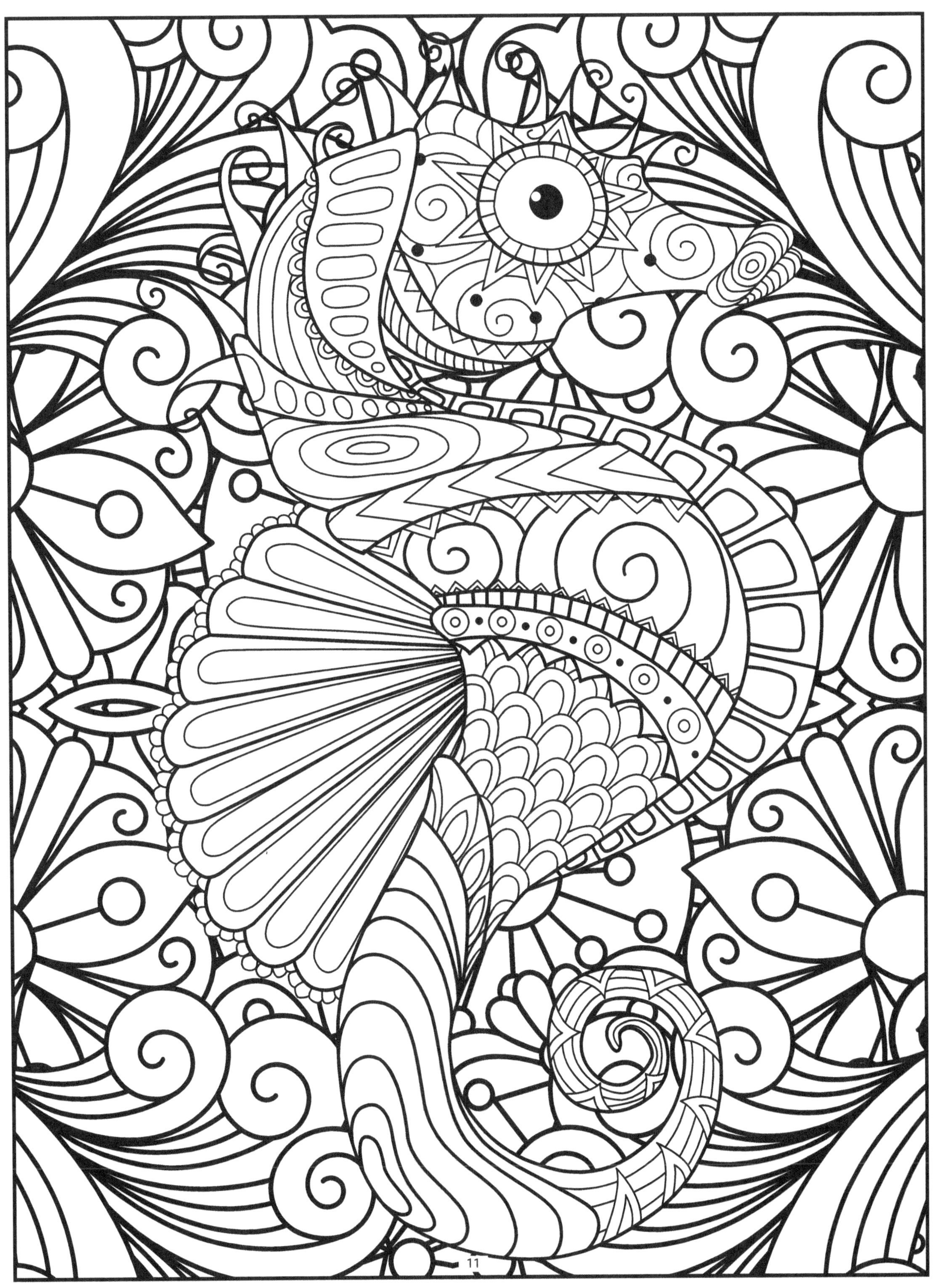

What Emotions Are Emerging as You Color?

What Symbolism or Significance Do You Attribute to the Colors You've Chose?

Can You Describe the Story or Narrative Behind Your Colorful Picture?

What new things come up from the old memories and experiences?

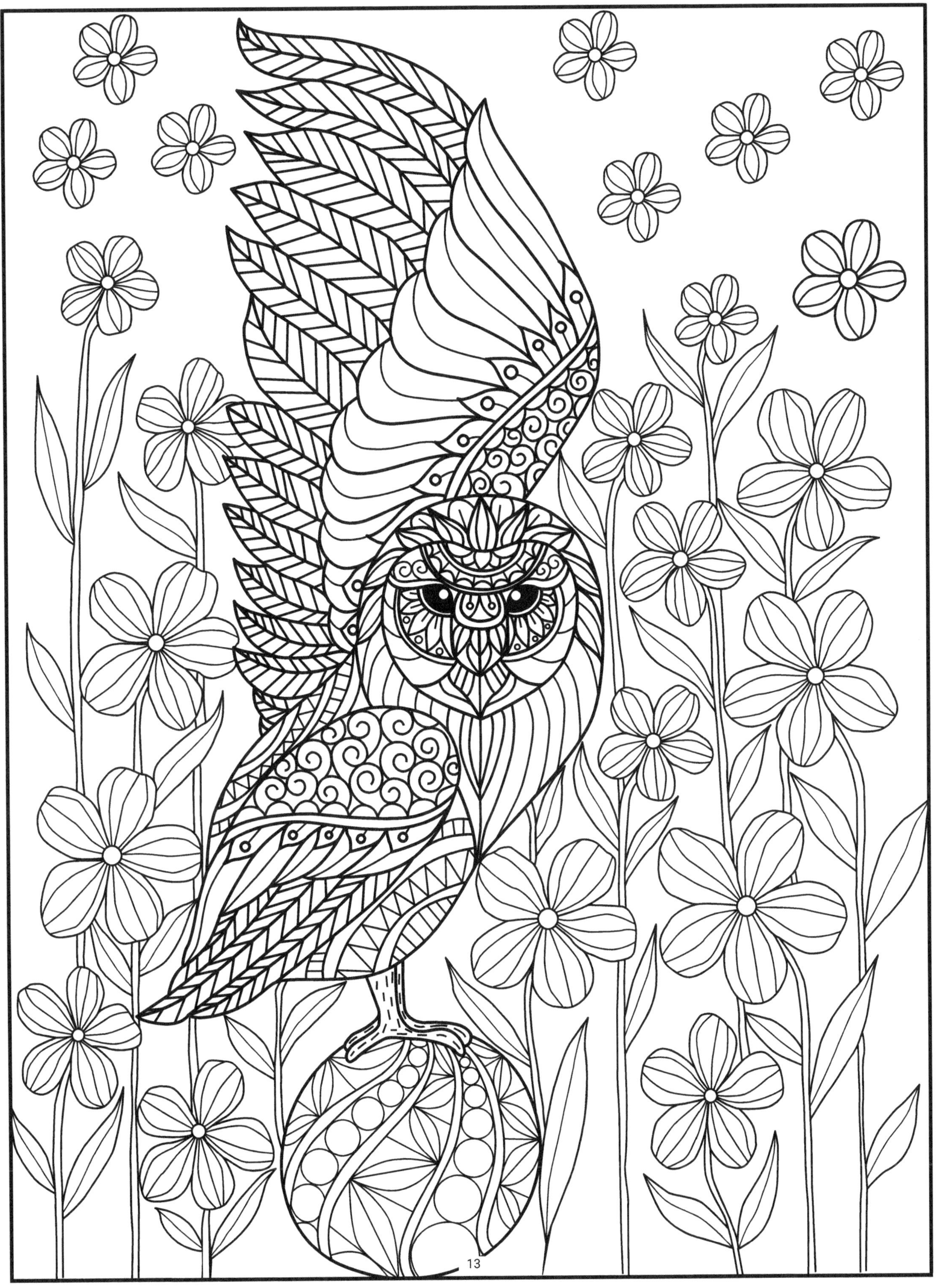

What Emotions Are Emerging as You Color?

What Symbolism or Significance Do You Attribute to the Colors You've Chose?

Can You Describe the Story or Narrative Behind Your Colorful Picture?

What new things come up from the old memories and experiences?

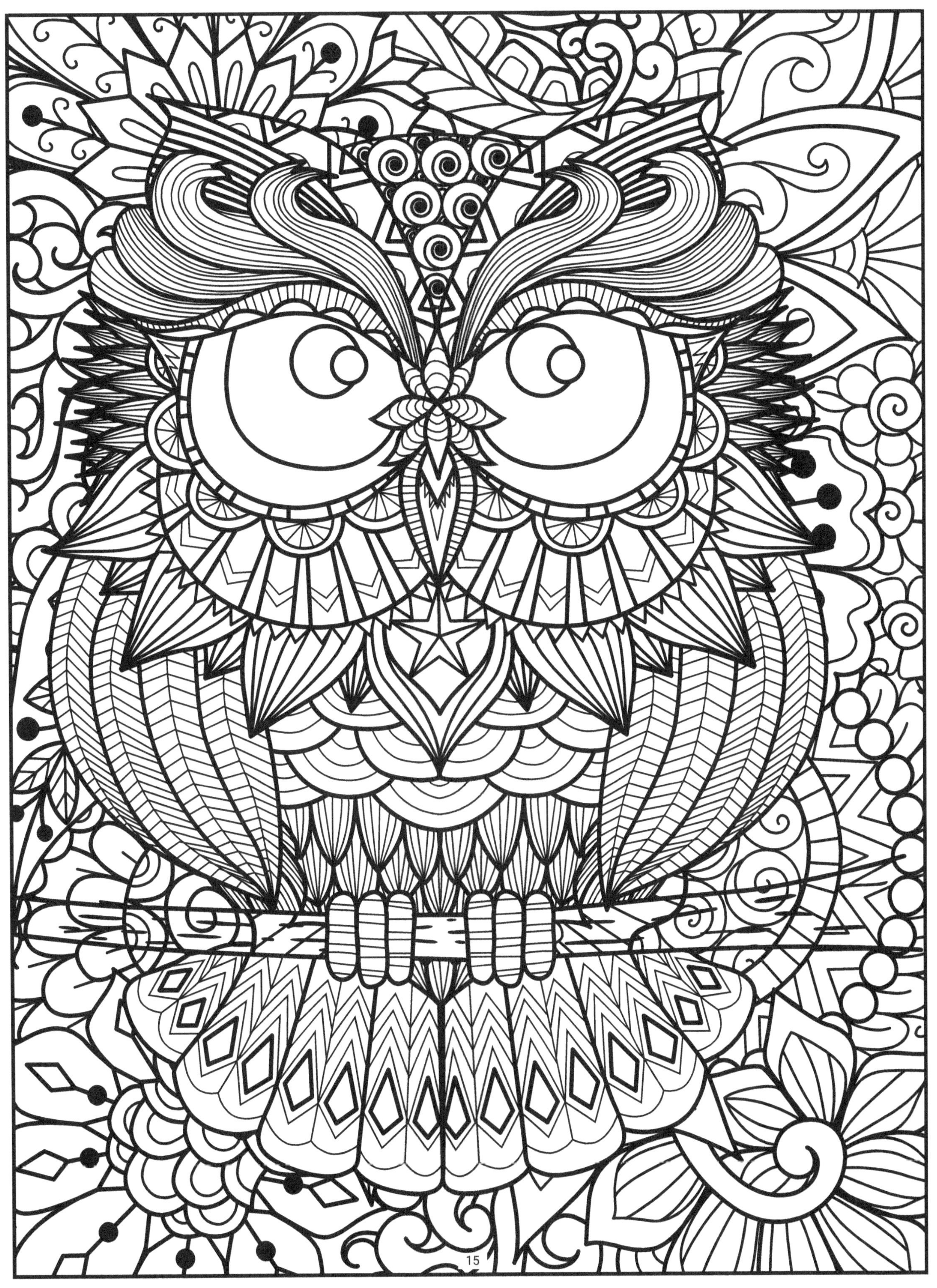

What Emotions Are Emerging as You Color?

What Symbolism or Significance Do You Attribute to the Colors You've Chose?

Can You Describe the Story or Narrative Behind Your Colorful Picture?

What new things come up from the old memories and experiences?

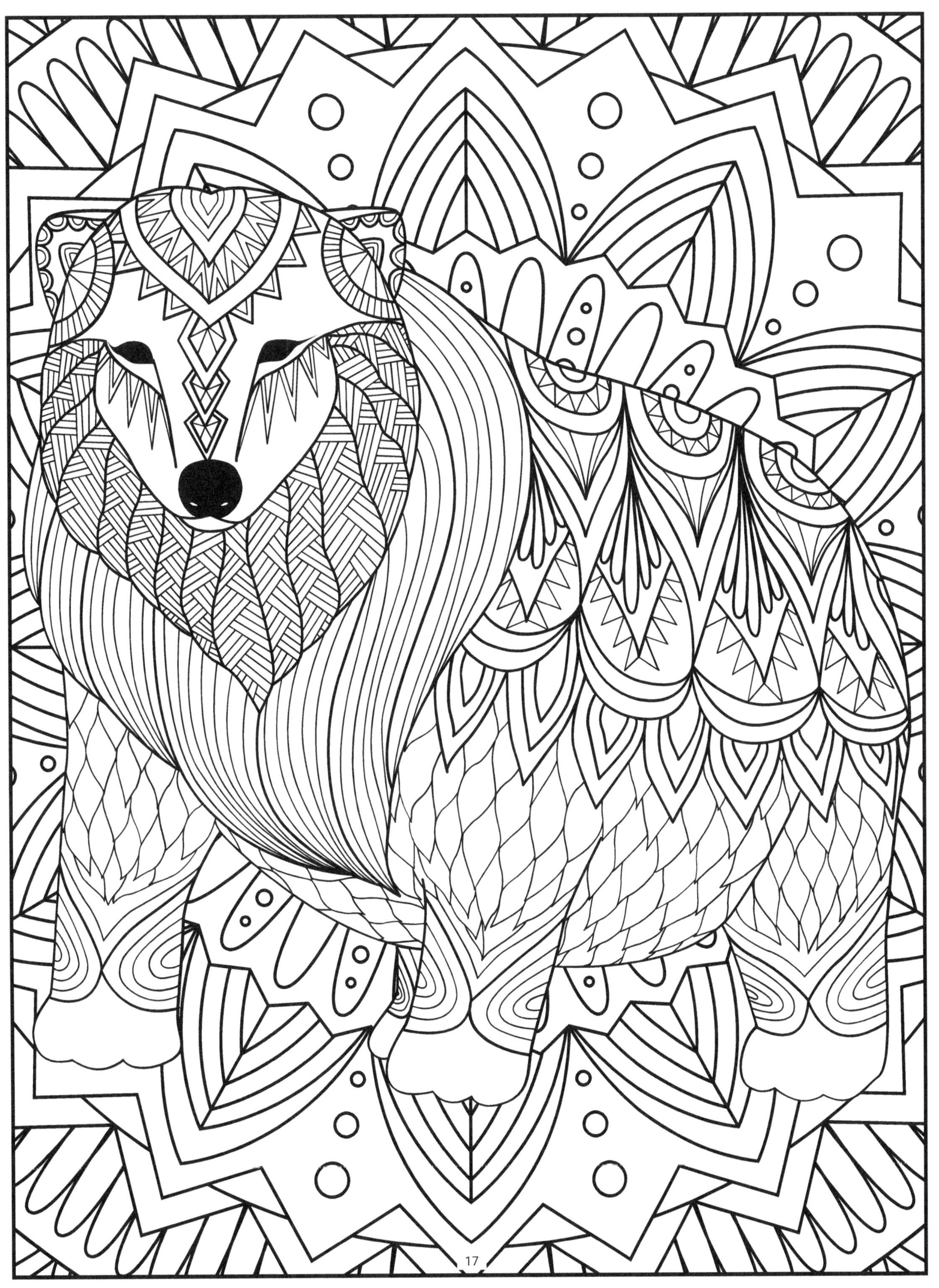

What Emotions Are Emerging as You Color?	**What Symbolism or Significance Do You Attribute to the Colors You've Chose?**
Can You Describe the Story or Narrative Behind Your Colorful Picture?	**What new things come up from the old memories and experiences?**

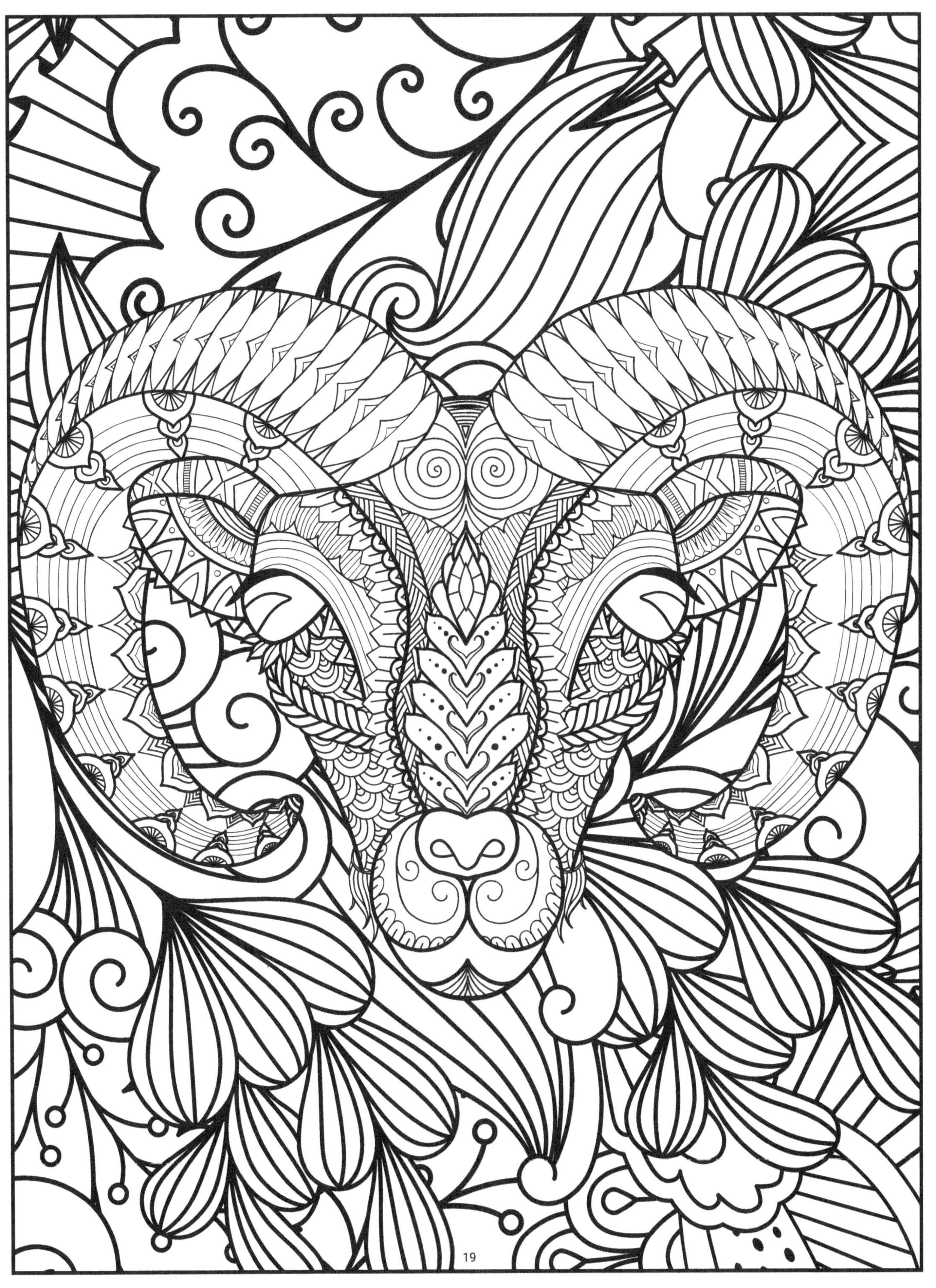

What Emotions Are Emerging as You Color?

What Symbolism or Significance Do You Attribute to the Colors You've Chose?

Can You Describe the Story or Narrative Behind Your Colorful Picture?

What new things come up from the old memories and experiences?

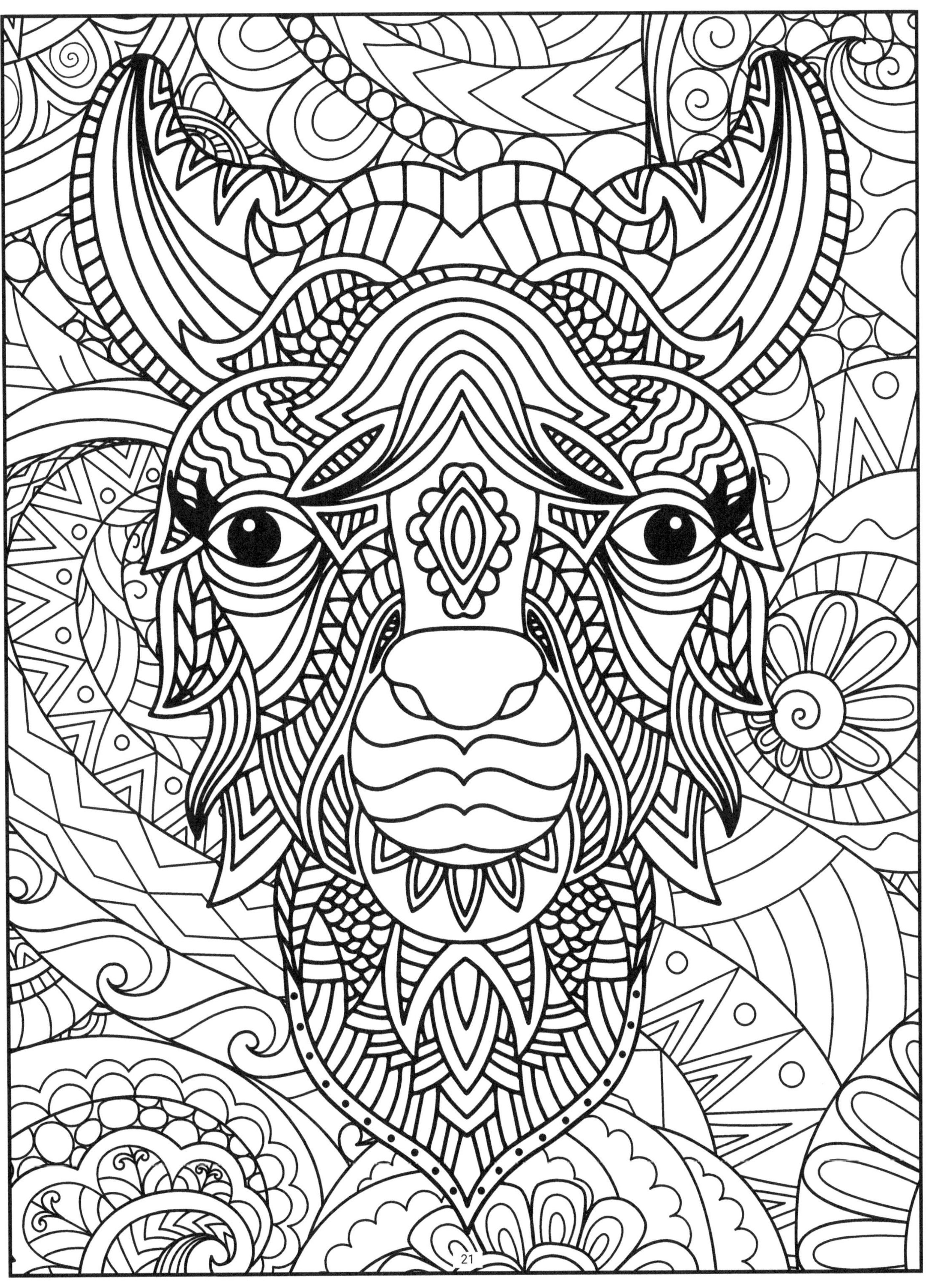

What Emotions Are Emerging as You Color?

What Symbolism or Significance Do You Attribute to the Colors You've Chose?

Can You Describe the Story or Narrative Behind Your Colorful Picture?

What new things come up from the old memories and experiences?

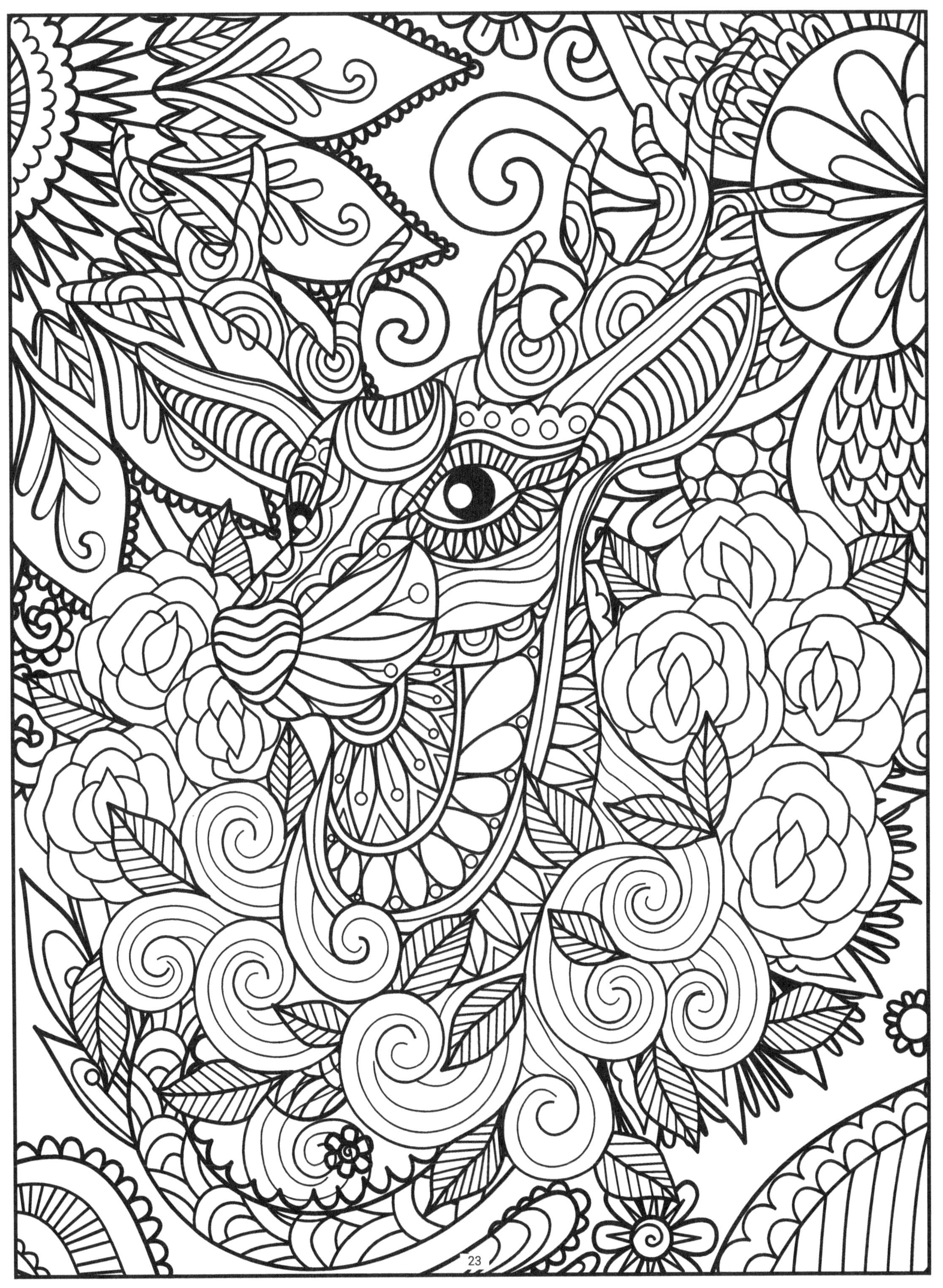

What Emotions Are Emerging as You Color?

What Symbolism or Significance Do You Attribute to the Colors You've Chose?

Can You Describe the Story or Narrative Behind Your Colorful Picture?

What new things come up from the old memories and experiences?

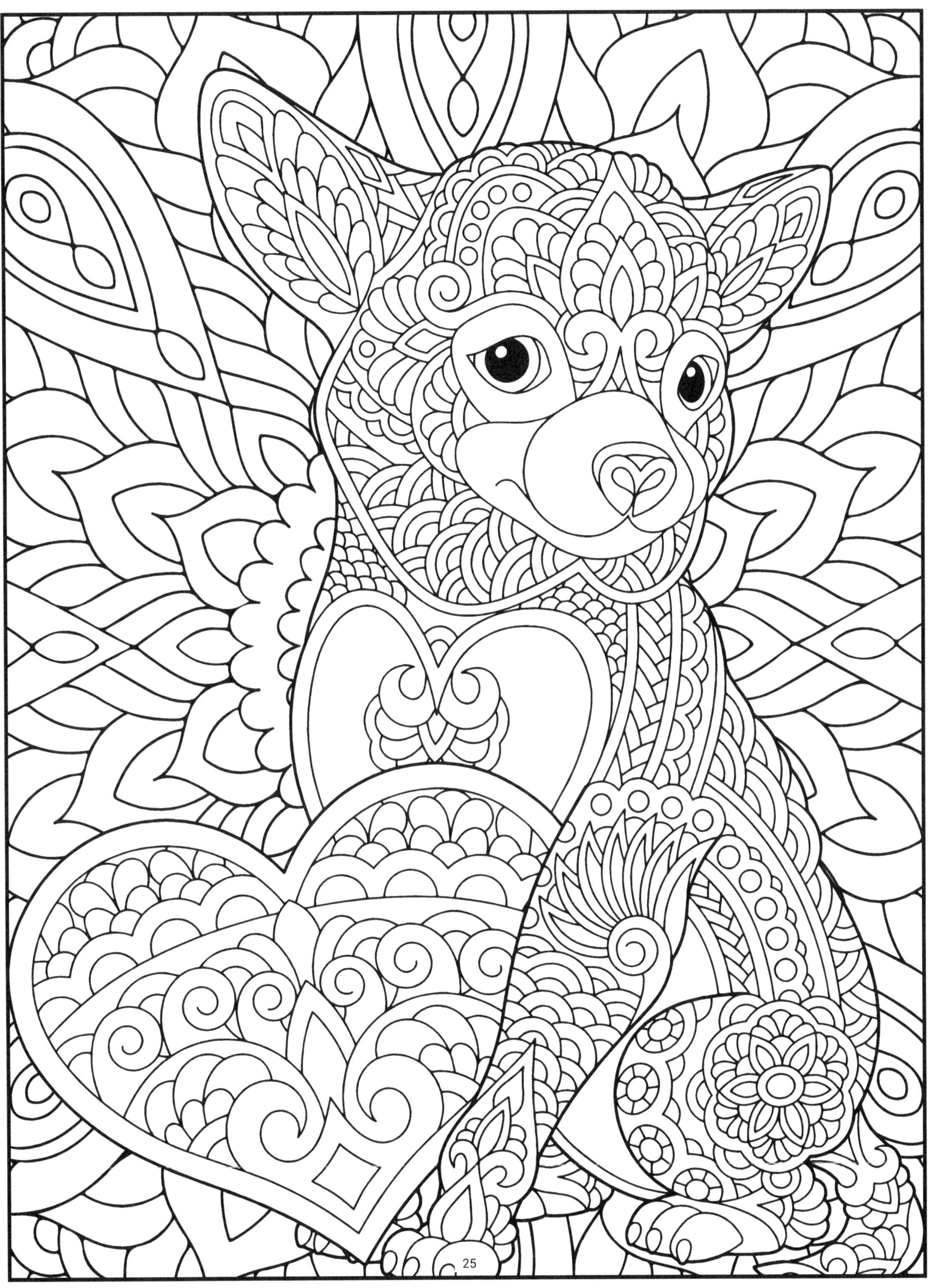

What Emotions Are Emerging as You Color?

What Symbolism or Significance Do You Attribute to the Colors You've Chose?

Can You Describe the Story or Narrative Behind Your Colorful Picture?

What new things come up from the old memories and experiences?

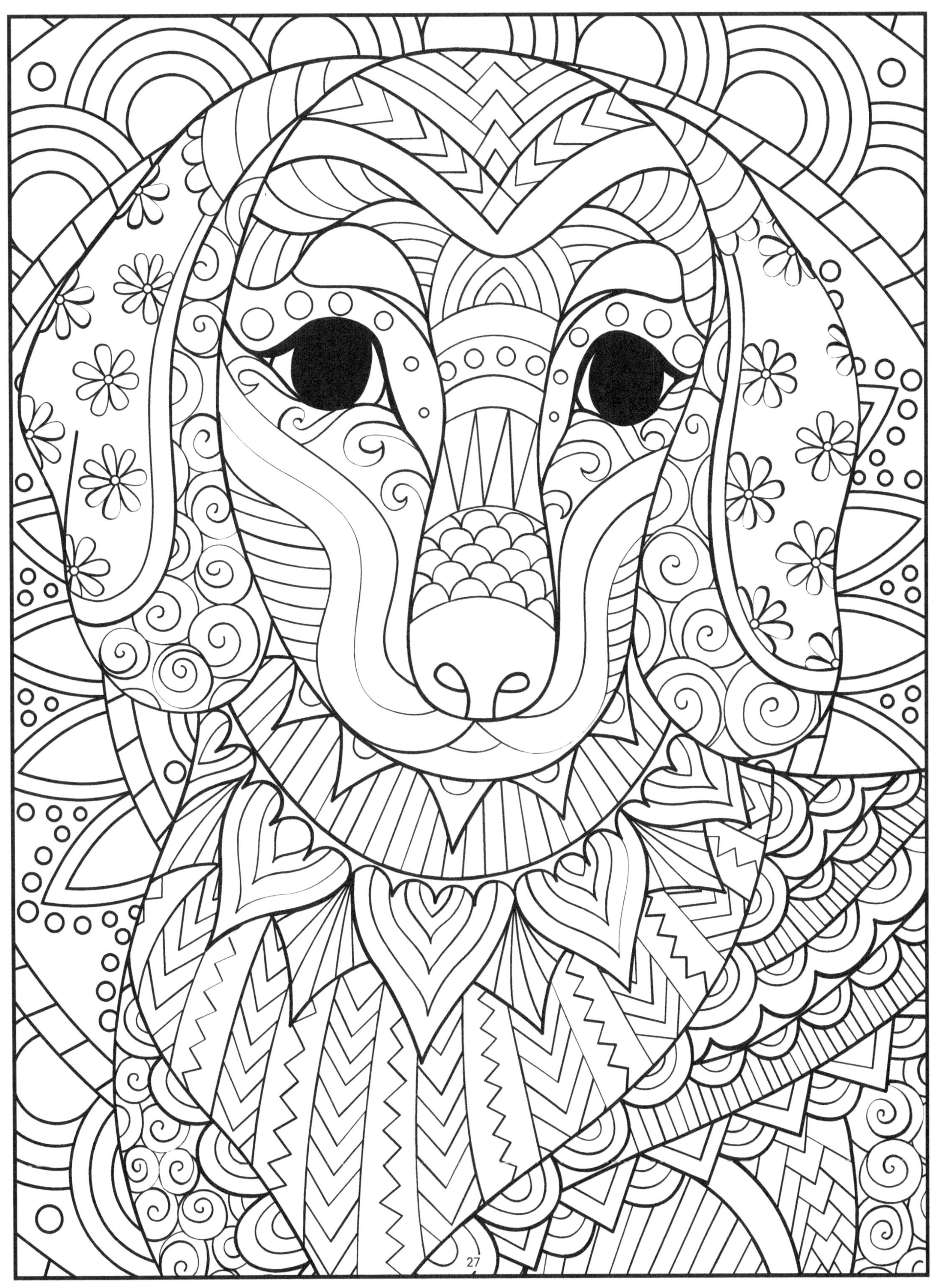

What Emotions Are Emerging as You Color?

What Symbolism or Significance Do You Attribute to the Colors You've Chose?

Can You Describe the Story or Narrative Behind Your Colorful Picture?

What new things come up from the old memories and experiences?

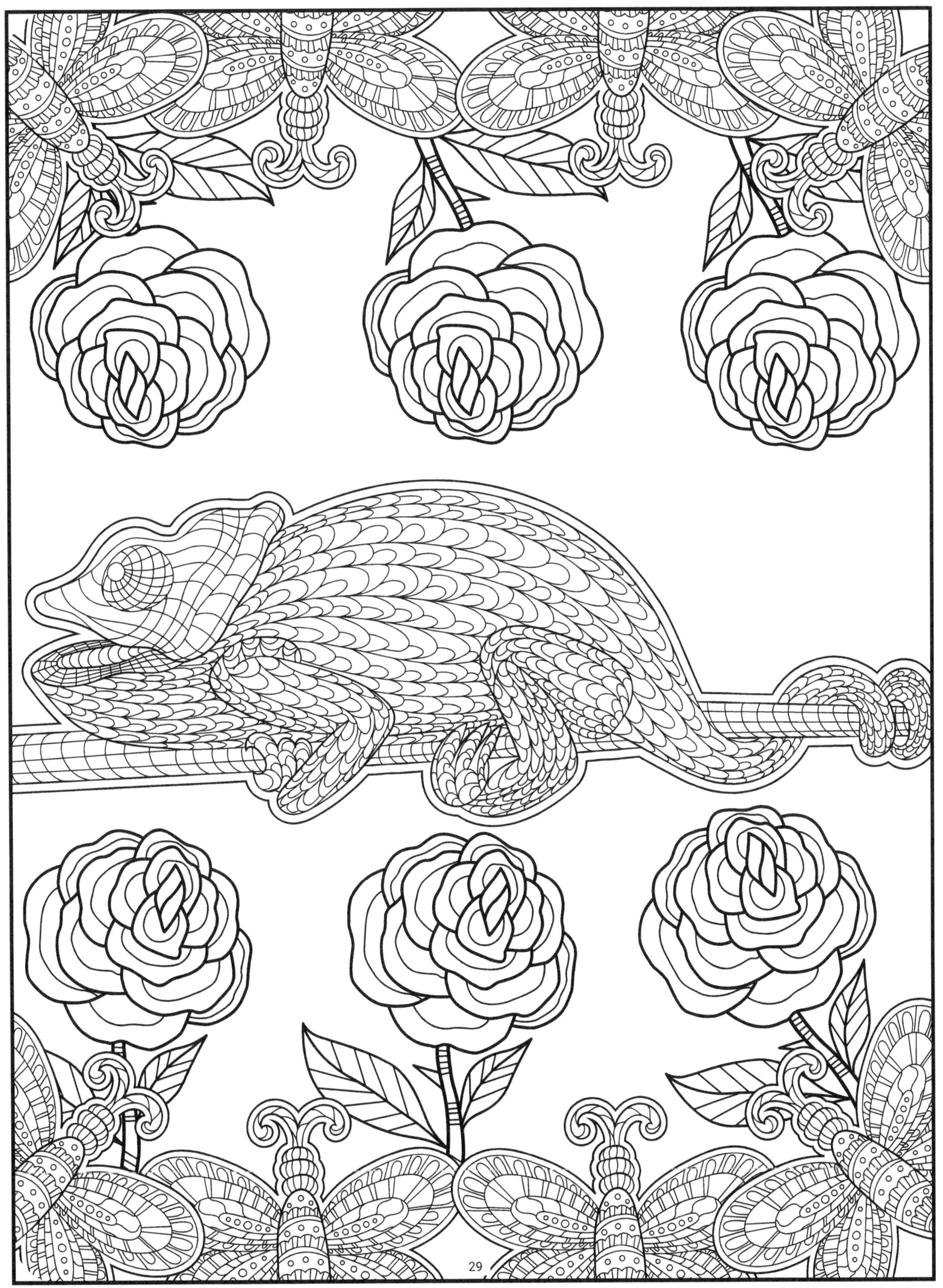

<table>
<tr><td>

What Emotions Are Emerging as You Color?

</td><td>

What Symbolism or Significance Do You Attribute to the Colors You've Chose?

</td></tr>
<tr><td>

Can You Describe the Story or Narrative Behind Your Colorful Picture?

</td><td>

What new things come up from the old memories and experiences?

</td></tr>
</table>

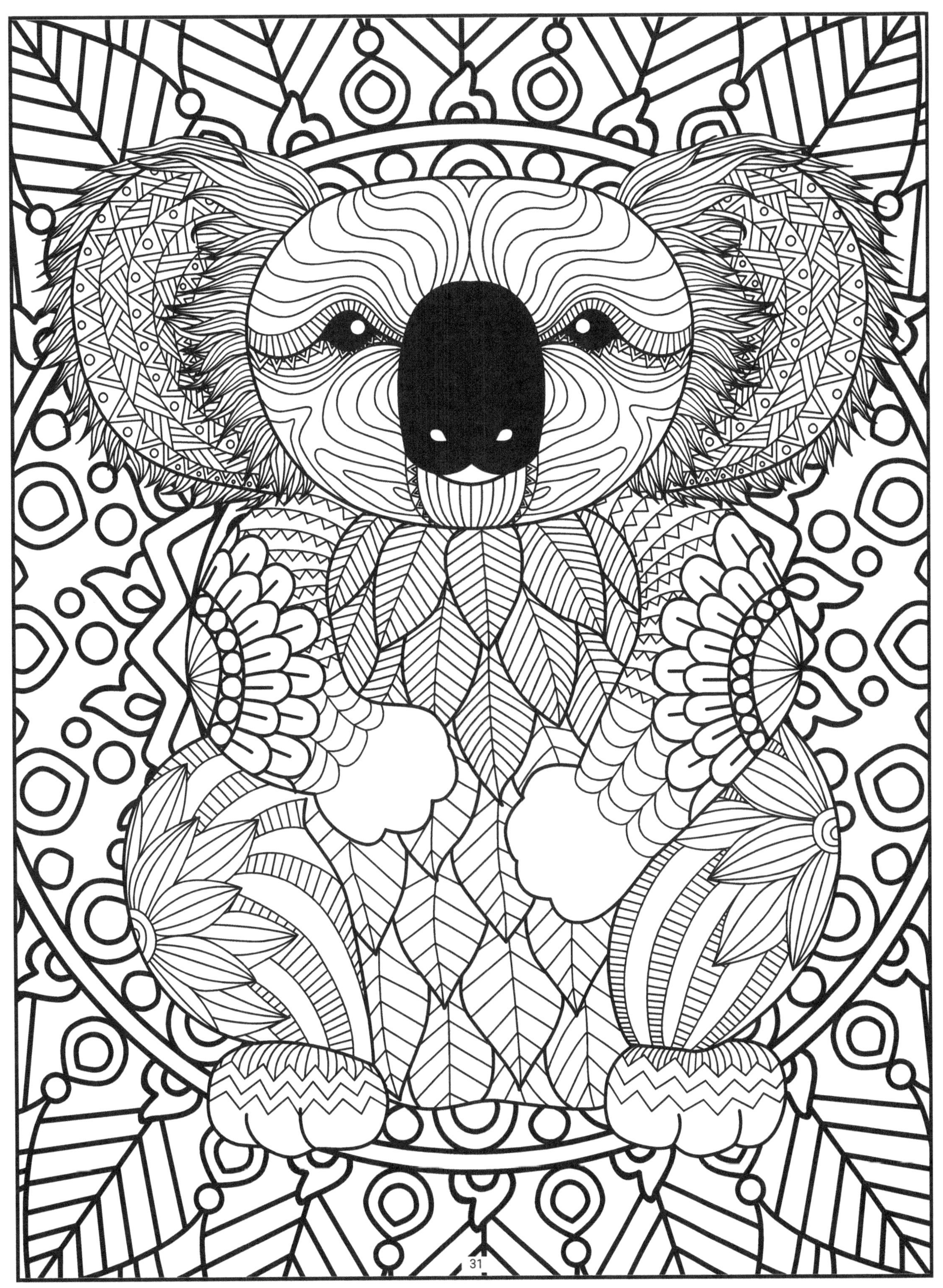

What Emotions Are Emerging as You Color?

What Symbolism or Significance Do You Attribute to the Colors You've Chose?

Can You Describe the Story or Narrative Behind Your Colorful Picture?

What new things come up from the old memories and experiences?

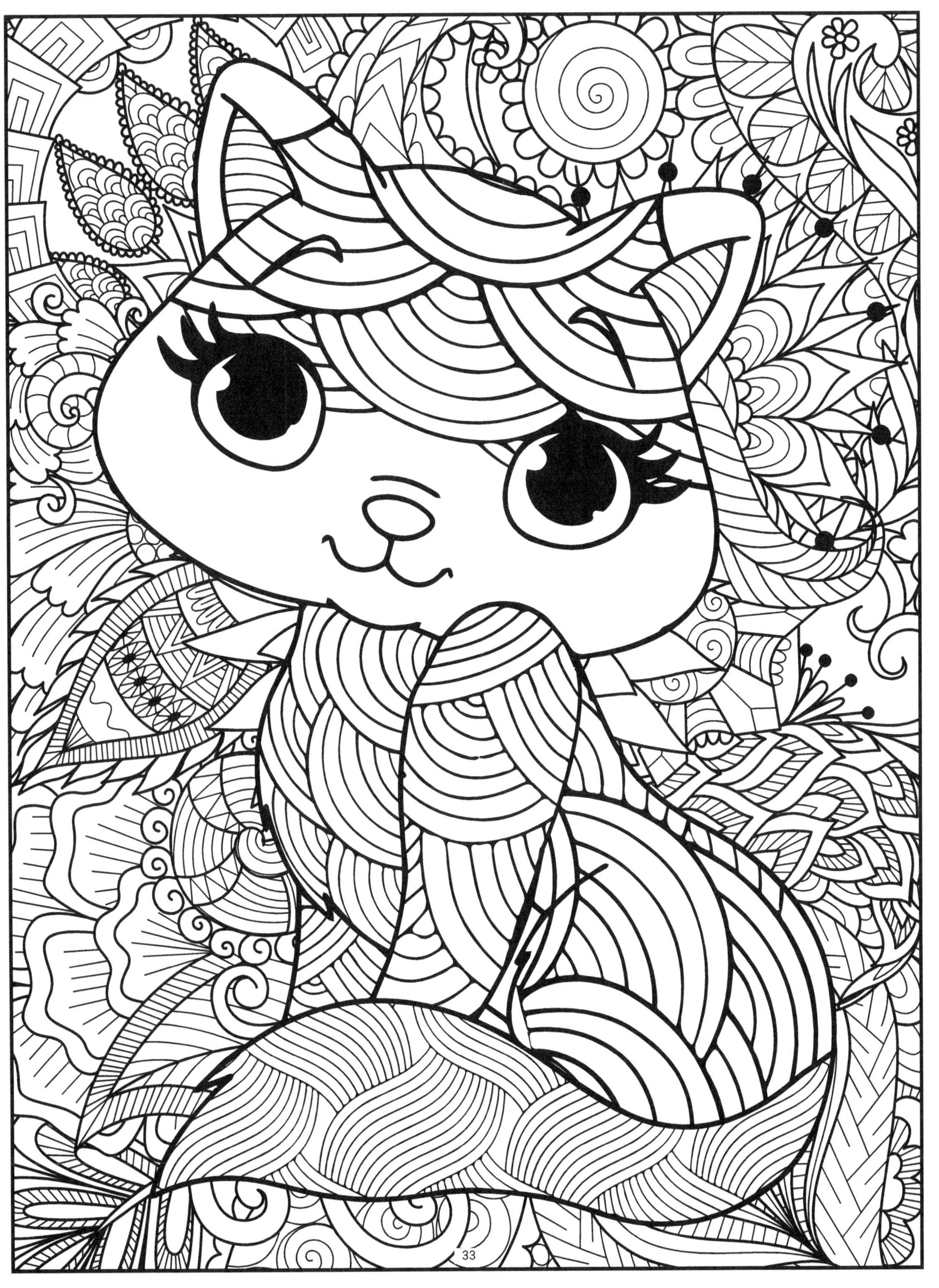

What Emotions Are Emerging as You Color?

What Symbolism or Significance Do You Attribute to the Colors You've Chose?

Can You Describe the Story or Narrative Behind Your Colorful Picture?

What new things come up from the old memories and experiences?

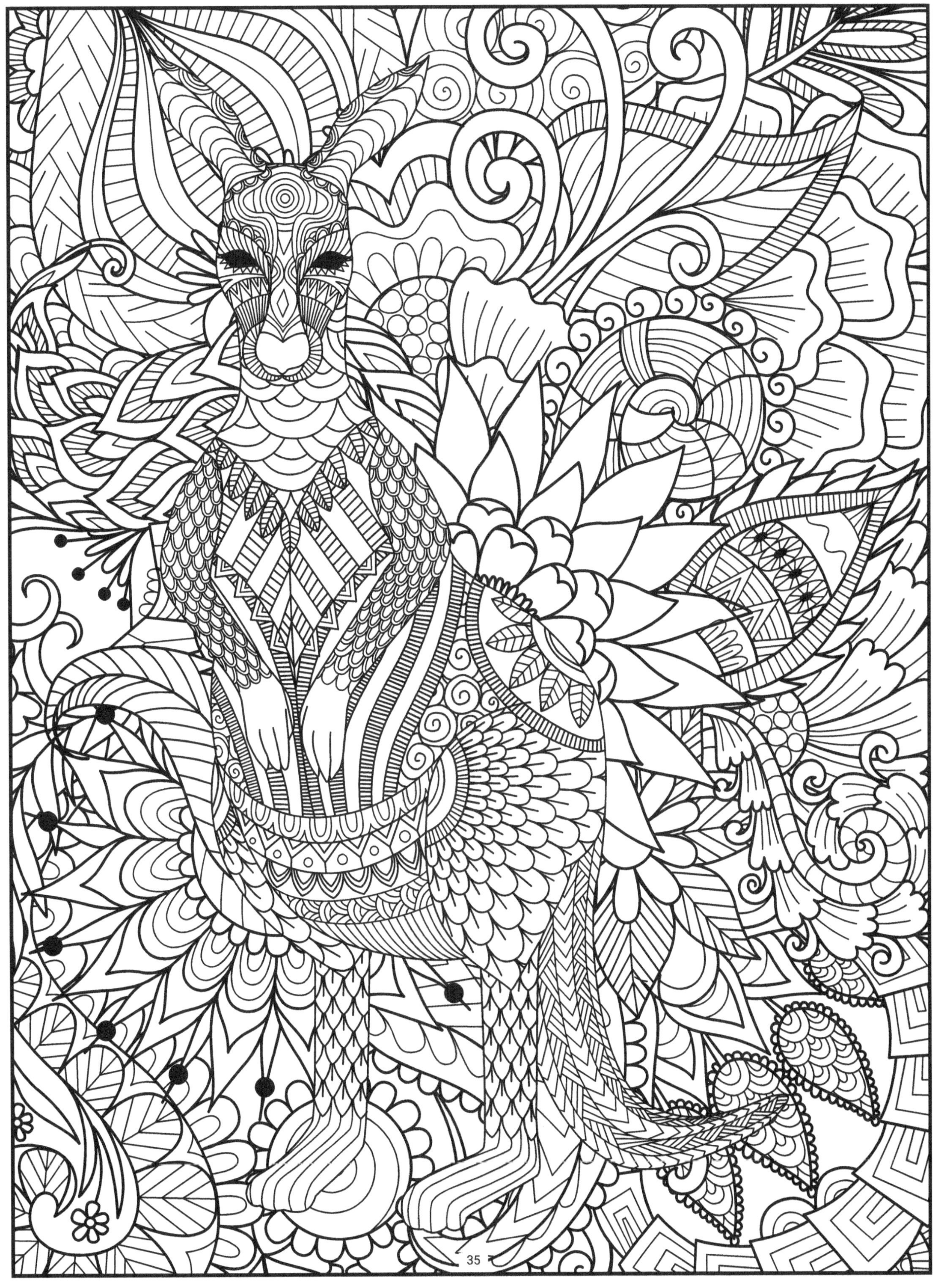

What Emotions Are Emerging as You Color?

What Symbolism or Significance Do You Attribute to the Colors You've Chose?

Can You Describe the Story or Narrative Behind Your Colorful Picture?

What new things come up from the old memories and experiences?

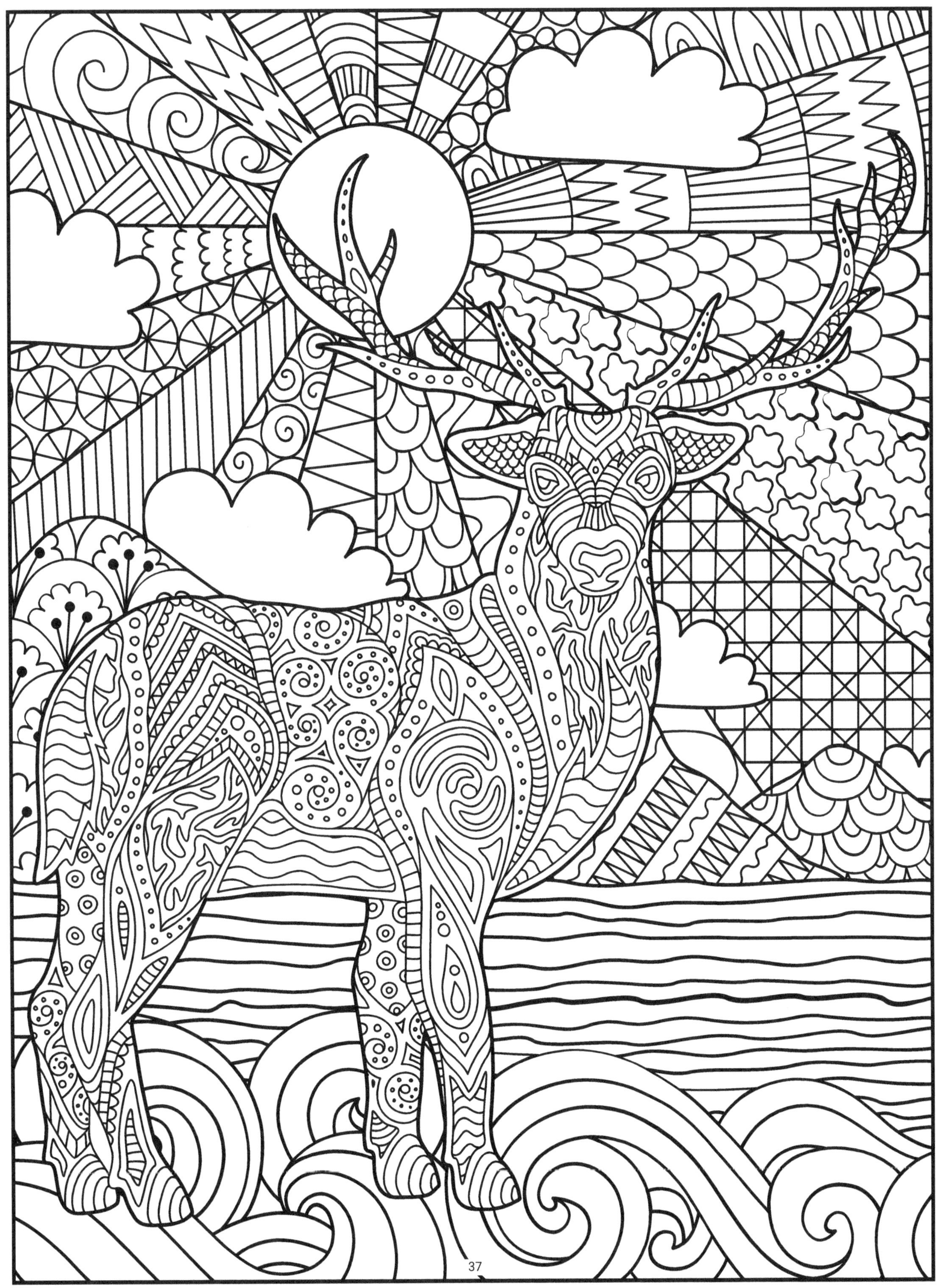

What Emotions Are Emerging as You Color?

What Symbolism or Significance Do You Attribute to the Colors You've Chose?

Can You Describe the Story or Narrative Behind Your Colorful Picture?

What new things come up from the old memories and experiences?

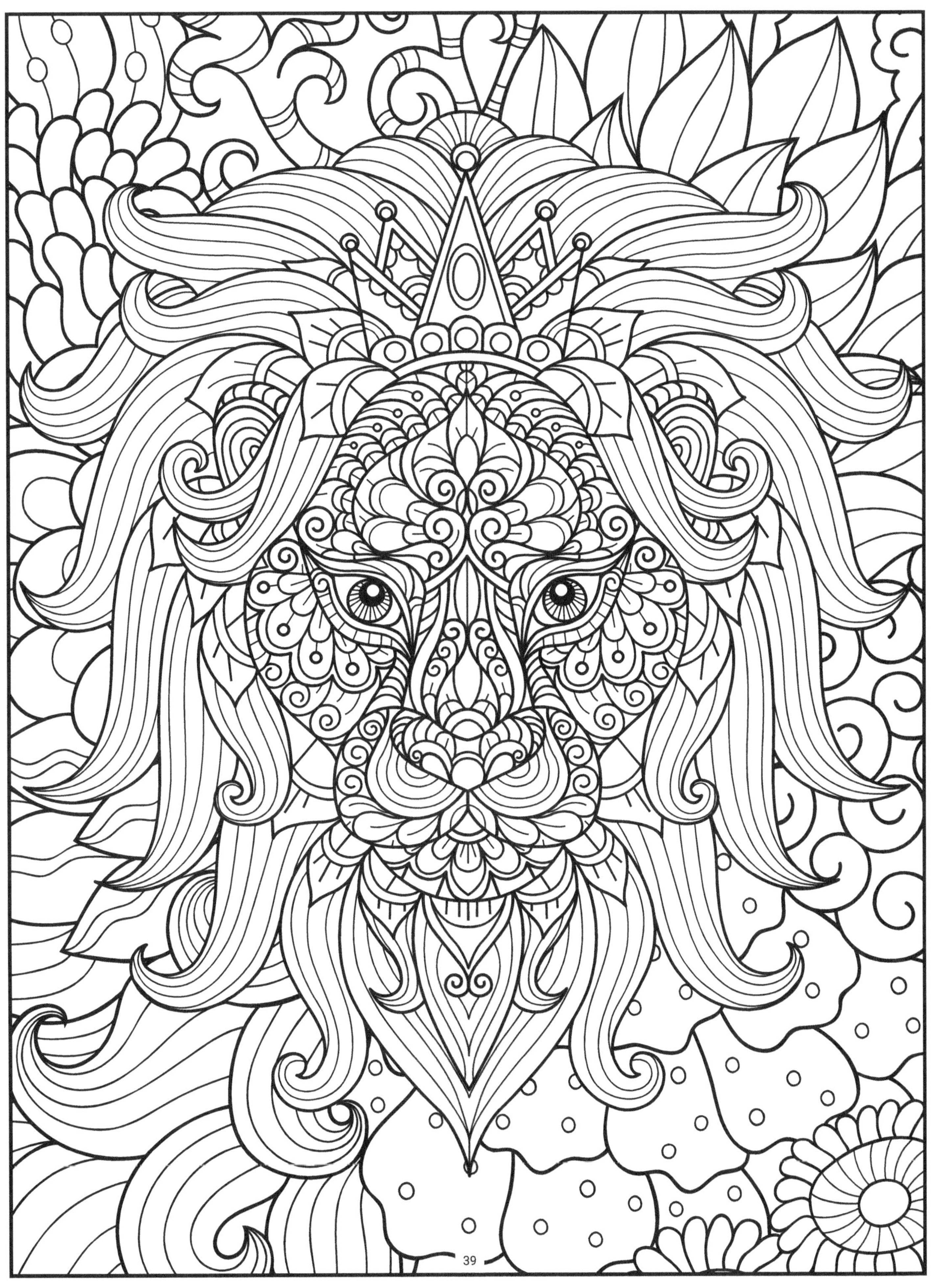

What Emotions Are Emerging as You Color?

What Symbolism or Significance Do You Attribute to the Colors You've Chose?

Can You Describe the Story or Narrative Behind Your Colorful Picture?

What new things come up from the old memories and experiences?

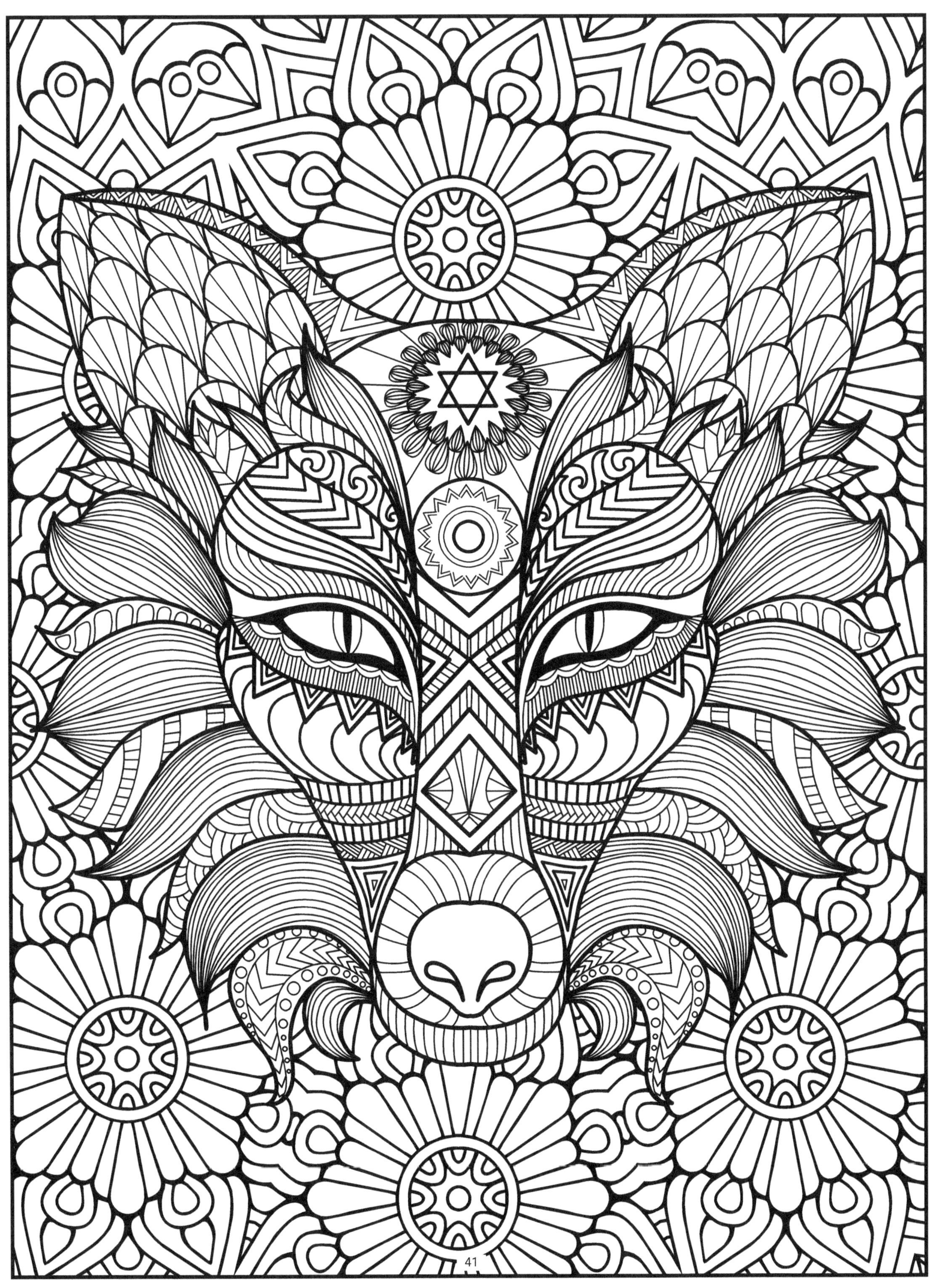

What Emotions Are Emerging as You Color?

What Symbolism or Significance Do You Attribute to the Colors You've Chose?

Can You Describe the Story or Narrative Behind Your Colorful Picture?

What new things come up from the old memories and experiences?

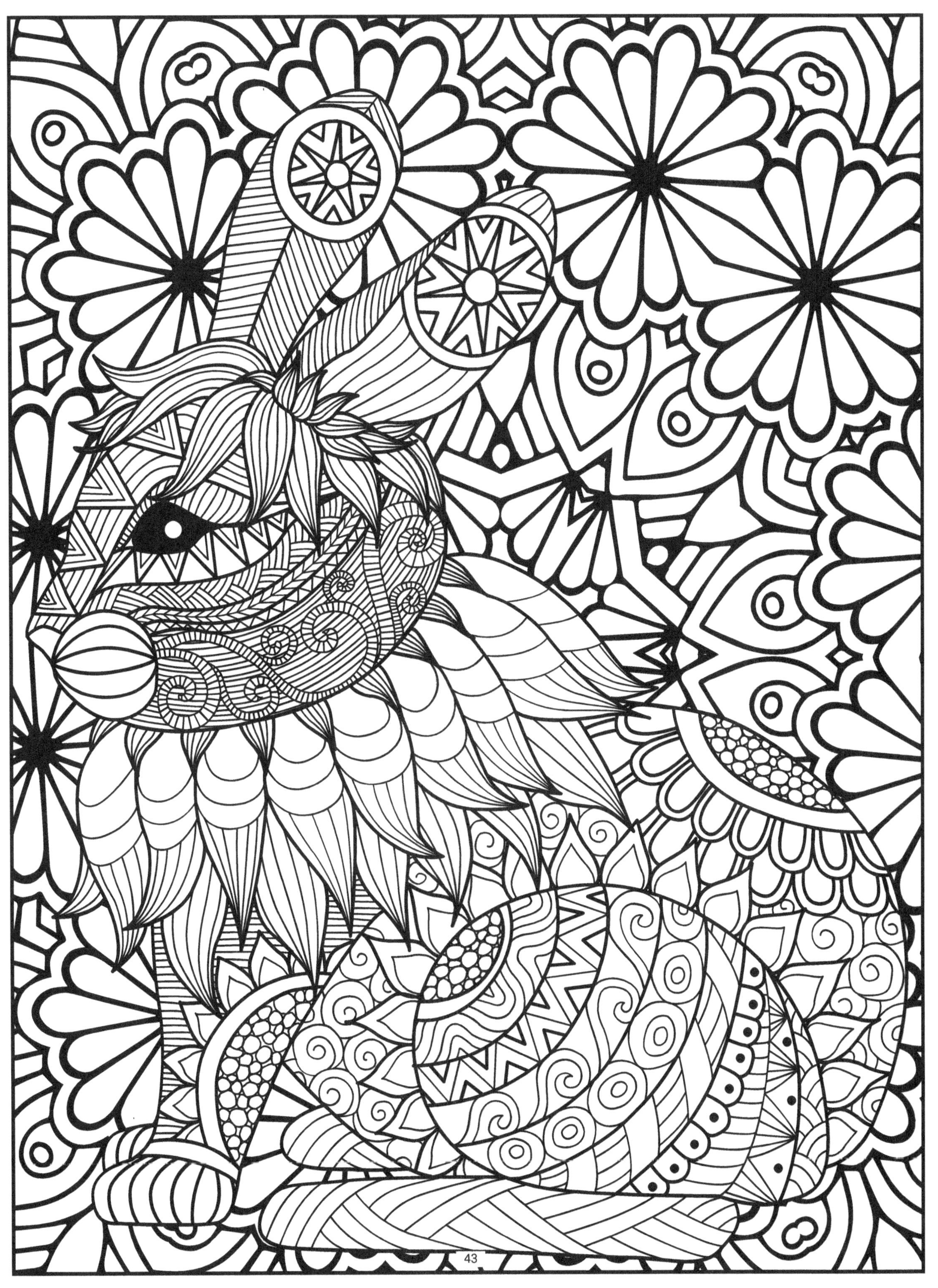

What Emotions Are Emerging as You Color?

What Symbolism or Significance Do You Attribute to the Colors You've Chose?

Can You Describe the Story or Narrative Behind Your Colorful Picture?

What new things come up from the old memories and experiences?

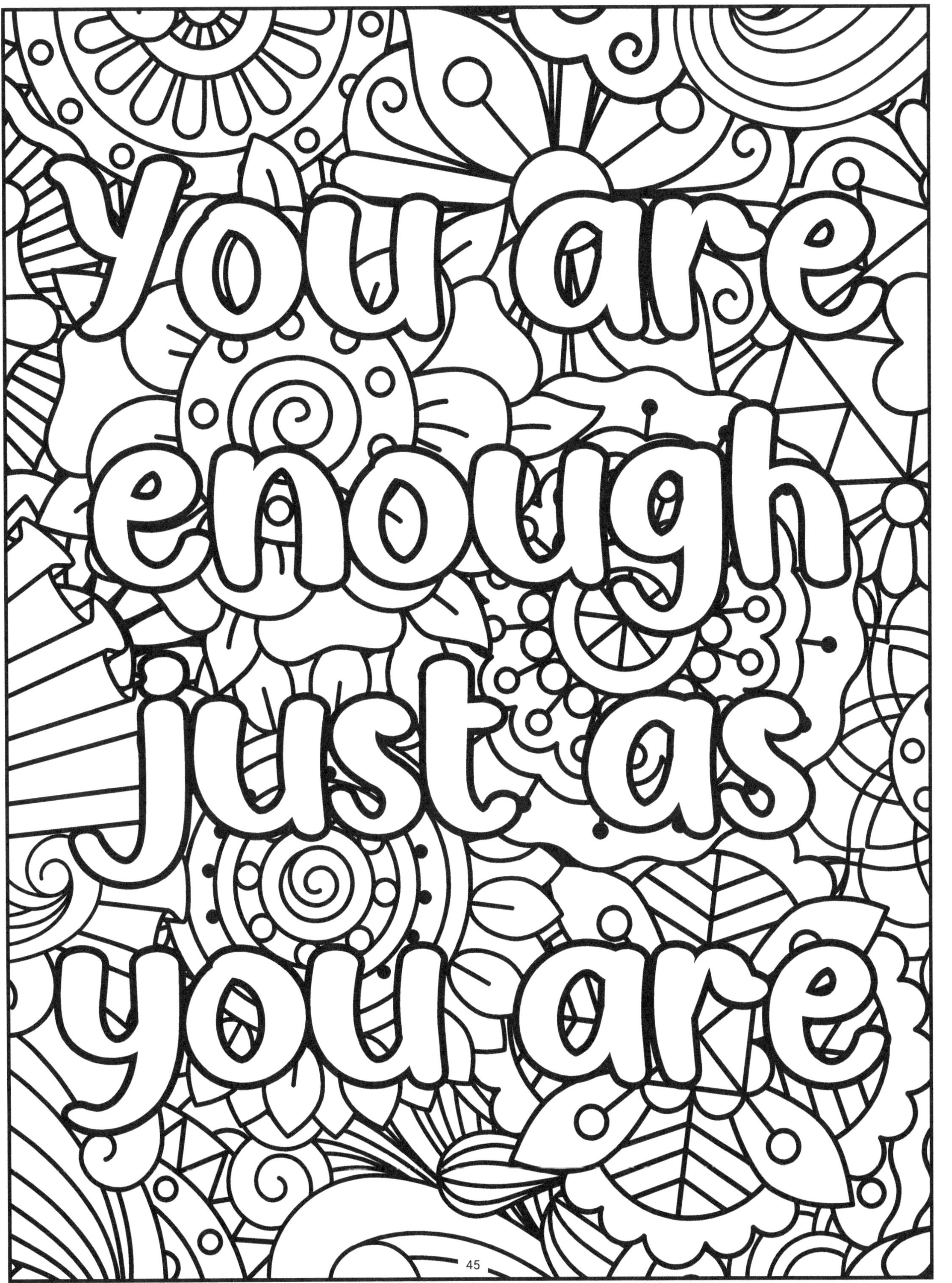

you are
enough
just as
you are

What Emotions Are Emerging as You Color?

What Symbolism or Significance Do You Attribute to the Colors You've Chose?

Can You Describe the Story or Narrative Behind Your Colorful Picture?

What new things come up from the old memories and experiences?

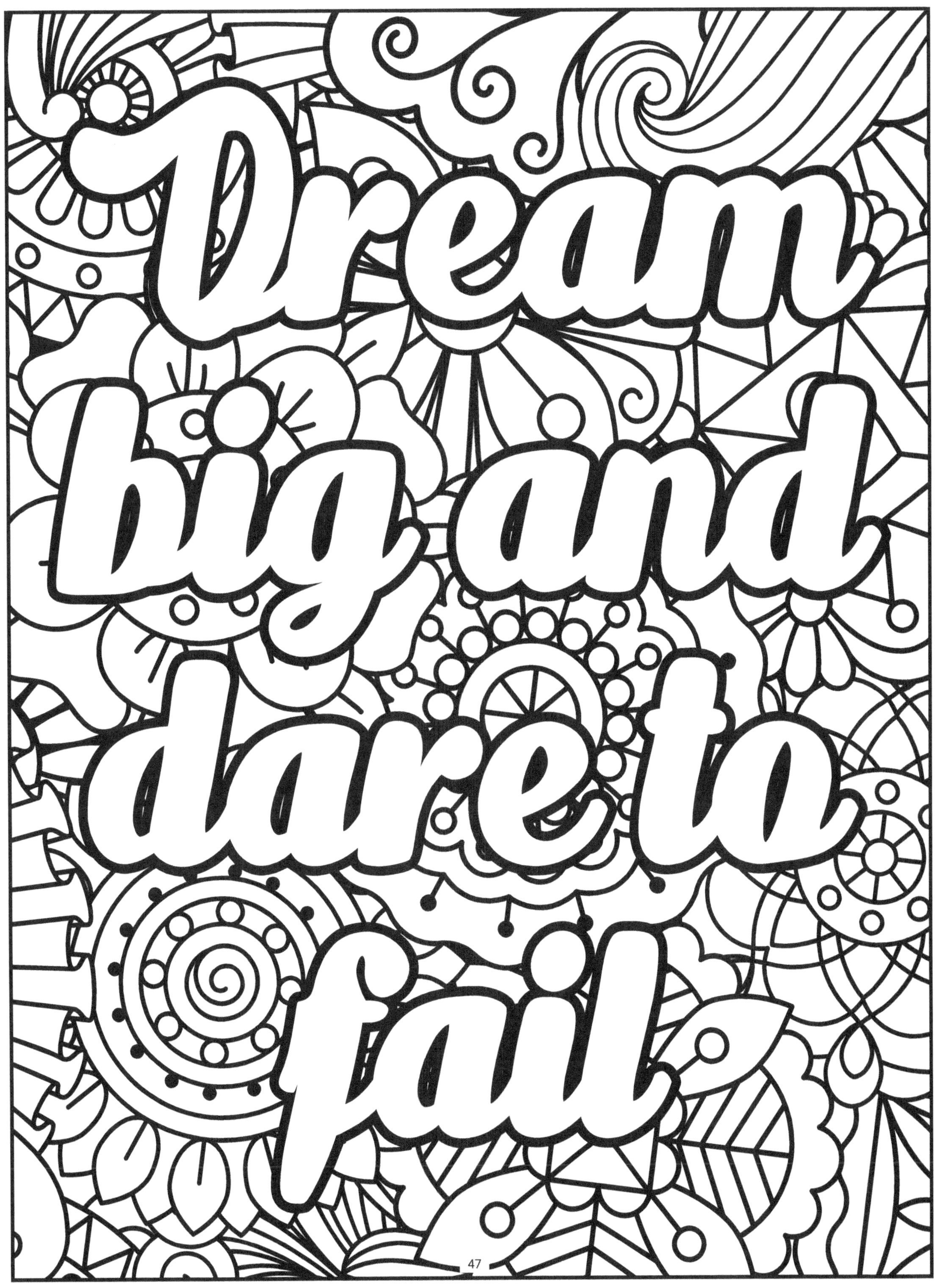

Dream
big and
dare to
fail

What Emotions Are Emerging as You Color?

What Symbolism or Significance Do You Attribute to the Colors You've Chose?

Can You Describe the Story or Narrative Behind Your Colorful Picture?

What new things come up from the old memories and experiences?

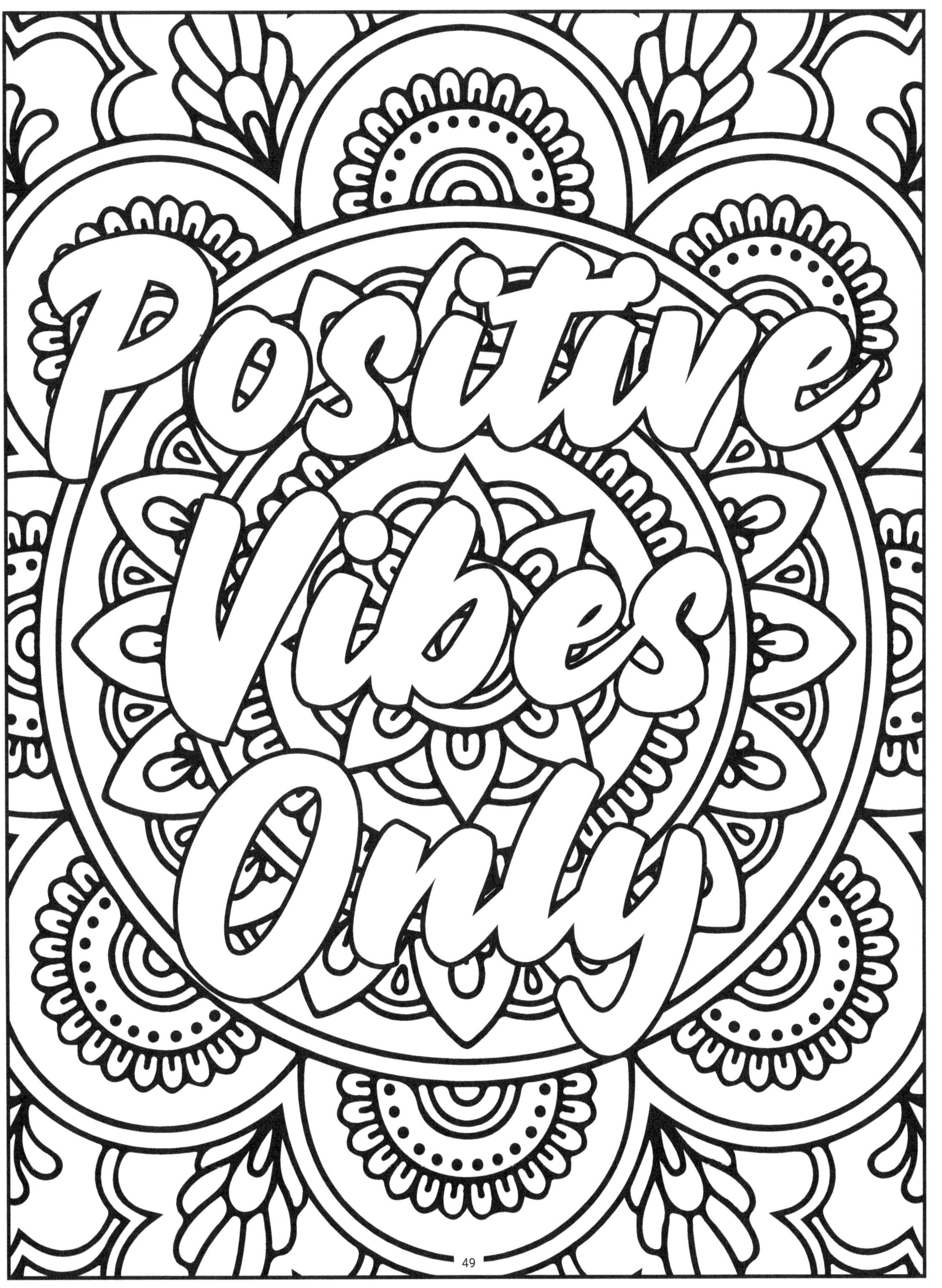

Positive Vibes Only

What Emotions Are Emerging as You Color?

What Symbolism or Significance Do You Attribute to the Colors You've Chose?

Can You Describe the Story or Narrative Behind Your Colorful Picture?

What new things come up from the old memories and experiences?

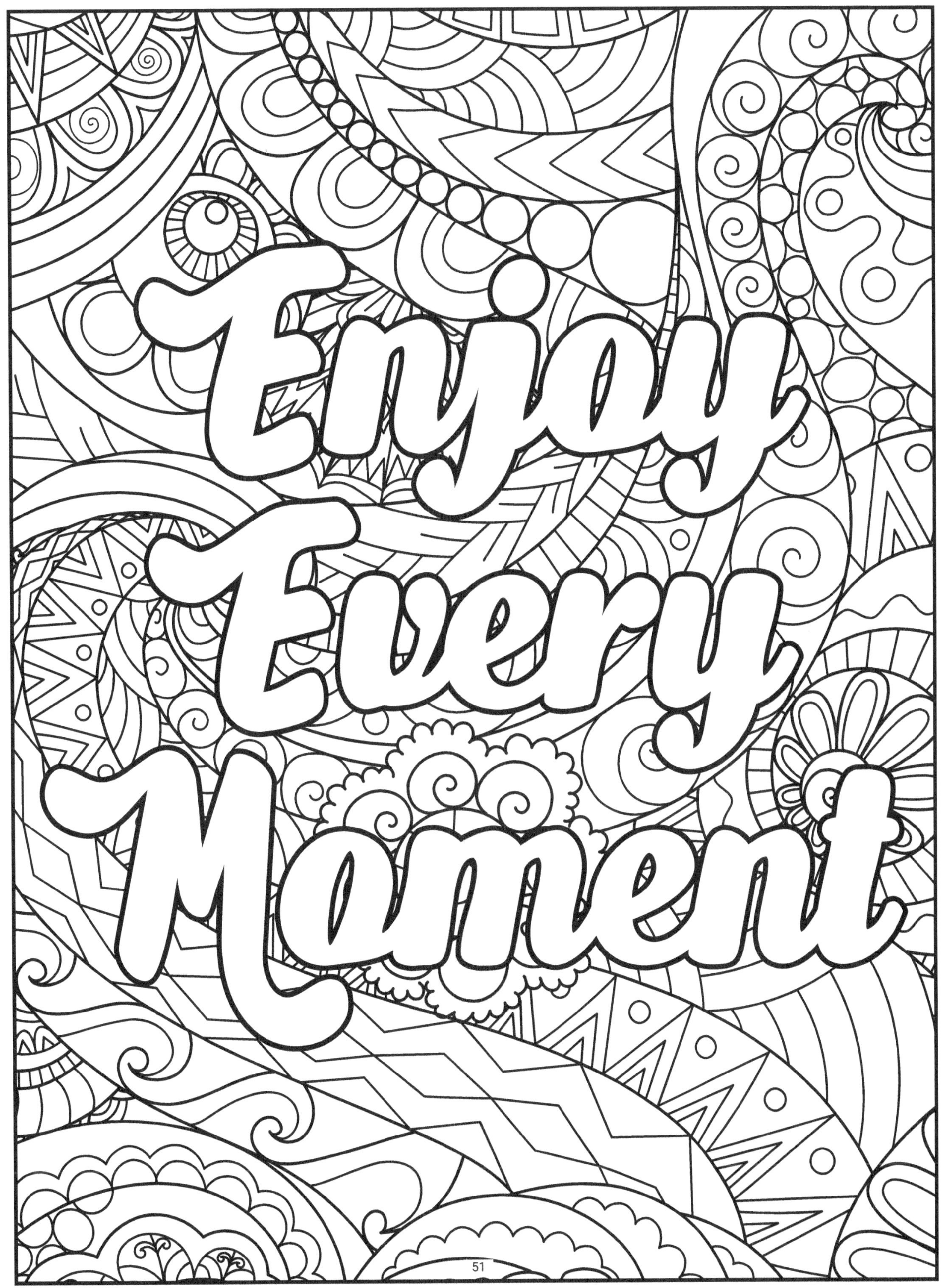
Enjoy
Every
Moment

What Emotions Are Emerging as You Color?

What Symbolism or Significance Do You Attribute to the Colors You've Chose?

Can You Describe the Story or Narrative Behind Your Colorful Picture?

What new things come up from the old memories and experiences?

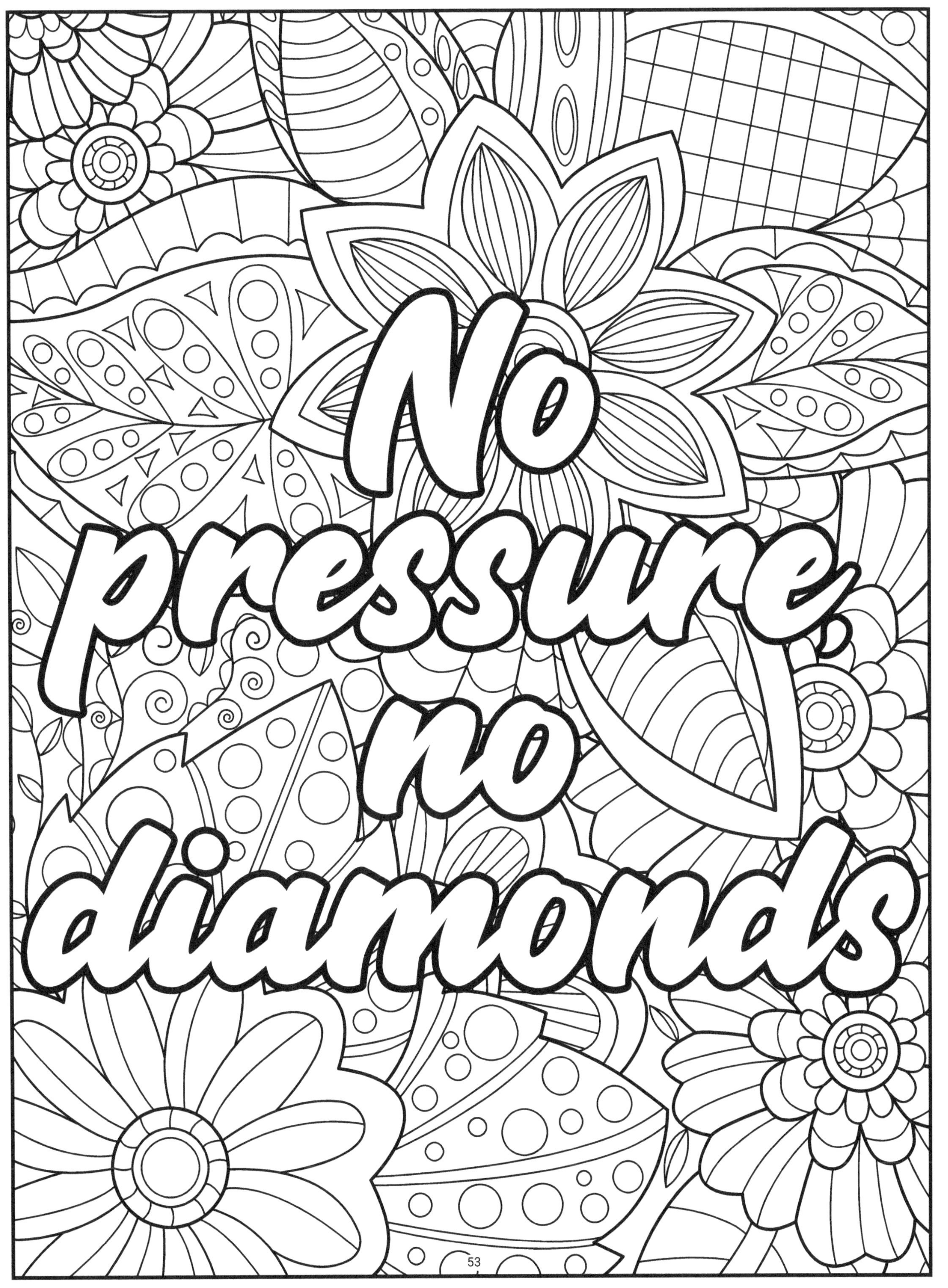
No pressure, no diamonds

What Emotions Are Emerging as You Color?

What Symbolism or Significance Do You Attribute to the Colors You've Chose?

Can You Describe the Story or Narrative Behind Your Colorful Picture?

What new things come up from the old memories and experiences?

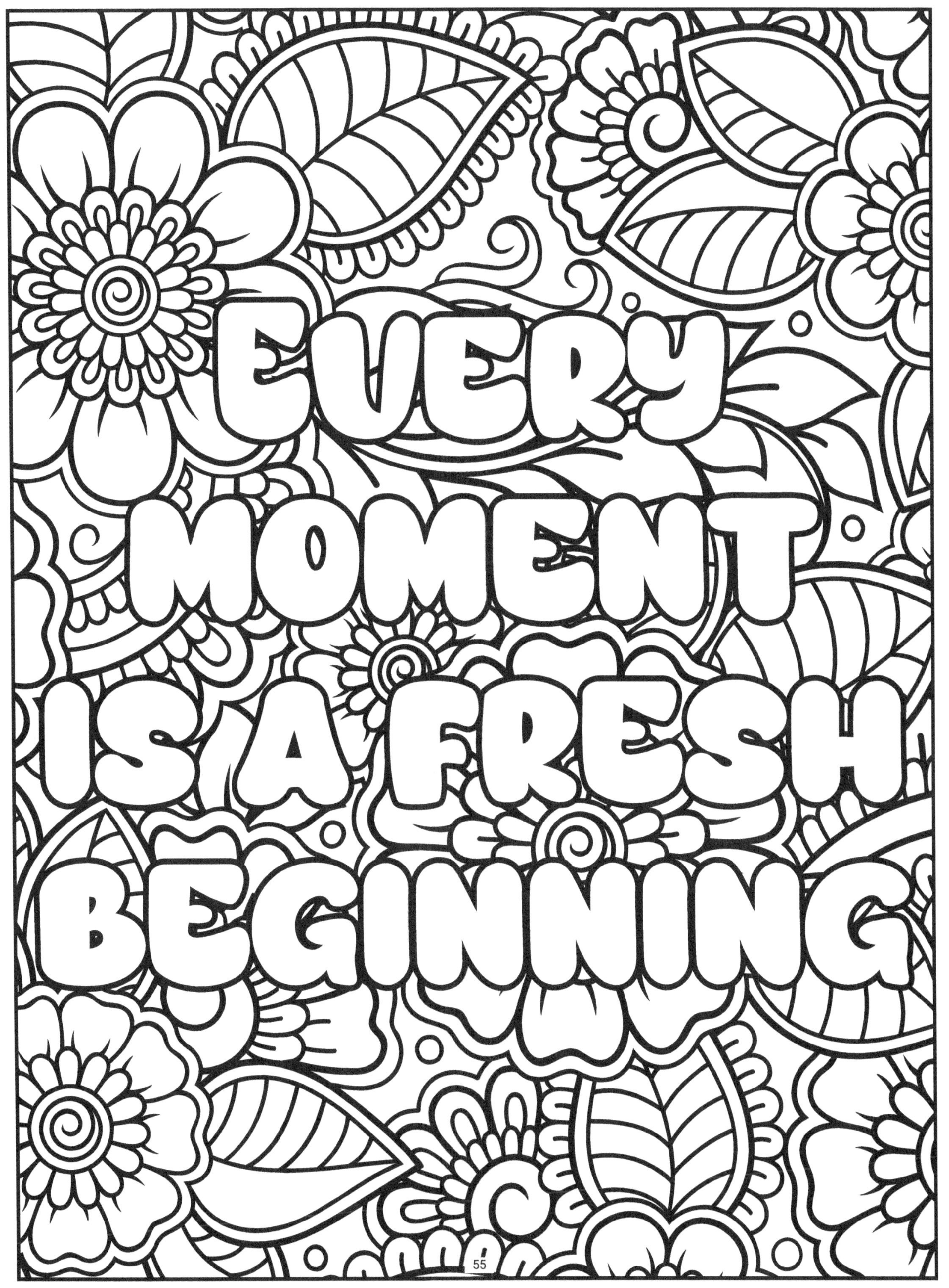

EVERY
MOMENT
IS A FRESH
BEGINNING

What Emotions Are Emerging as You Color?

What Symbolism or Significance Do You Attribute to the Colors You've Chose?

Can You Describe the Story or Narrative Behind Your Colorful Picture?

What new things come up from the old memories and experiences?

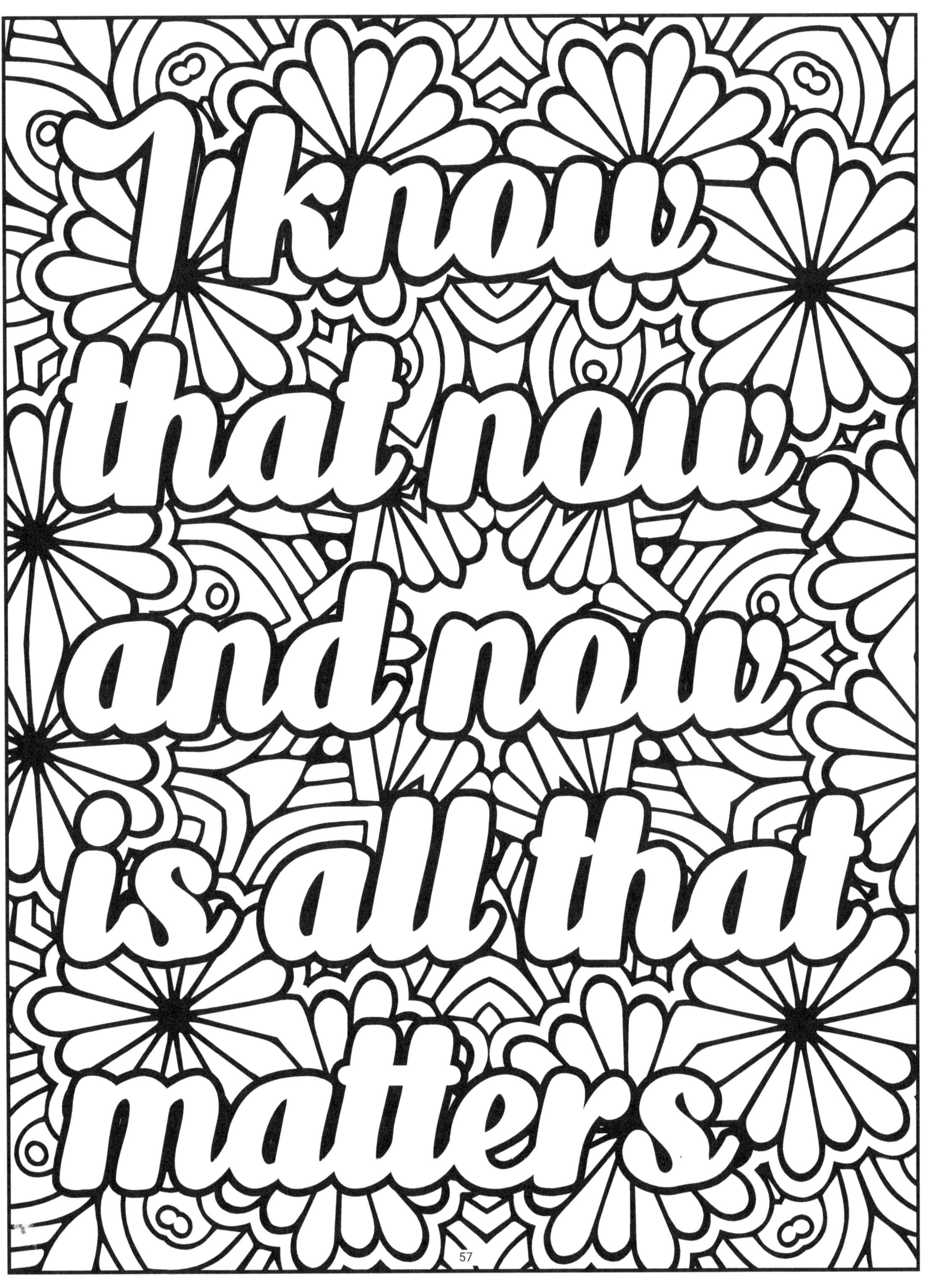

I know
that now,
and now
is all that
matters

What Emotions Are Emerging as You Color?

What Symbolism or Significance Do You Attribute to the Colors You've Chose?

Can You Describe the Story or Narrative Behind Your Colorful Picture?

What new things come up from the old memories and experiences?

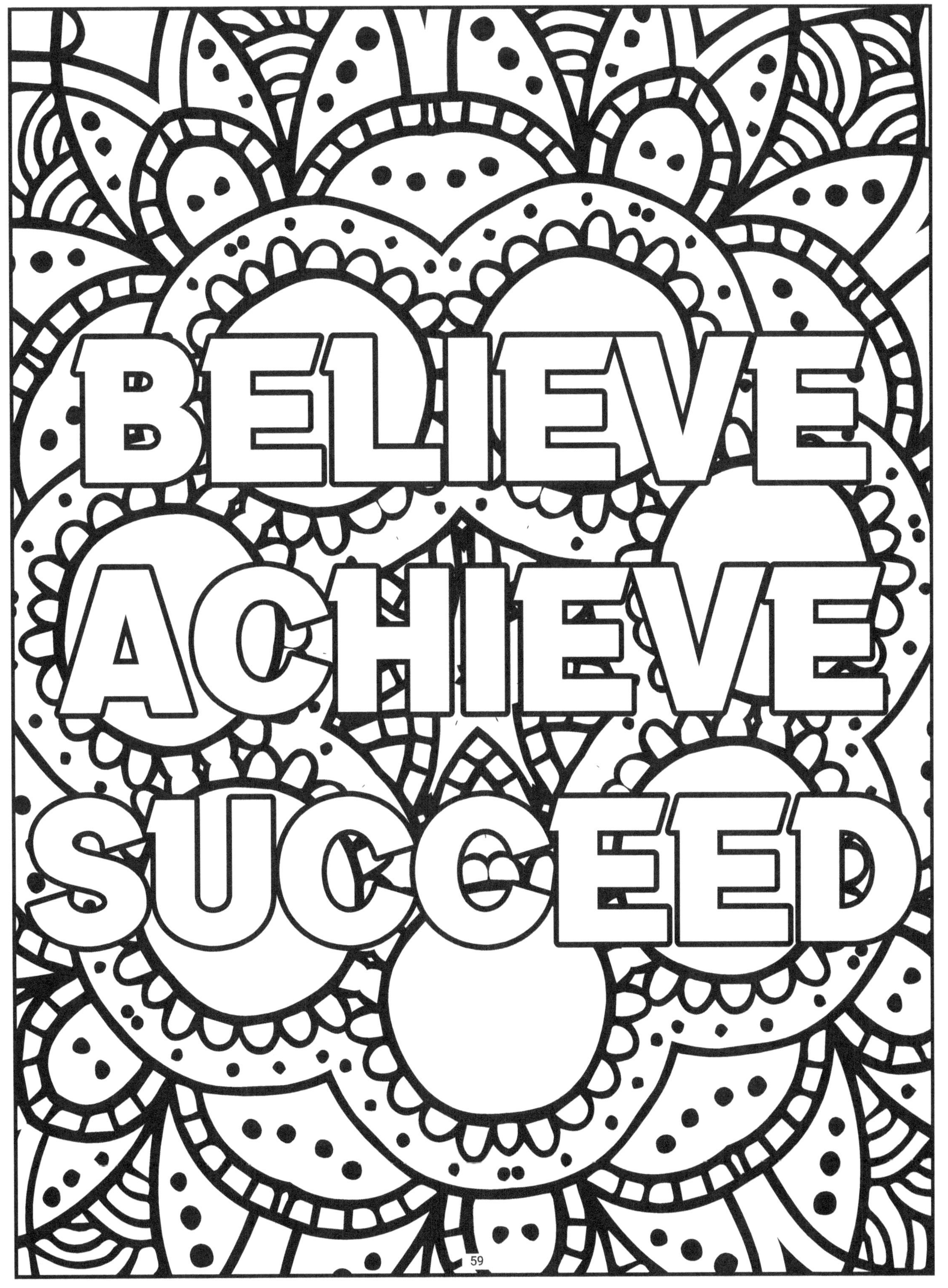

BELIEVE
ACHIEVE
SUCCEED

What Emotions Are Emerging as You Color?

What Symbolism or Significance Do You Attribute to the Colors You've Chose?

Can You Describe the Story or Narrative Behind Your Colorful Picture?

What new things come up from the old memories and experiences?

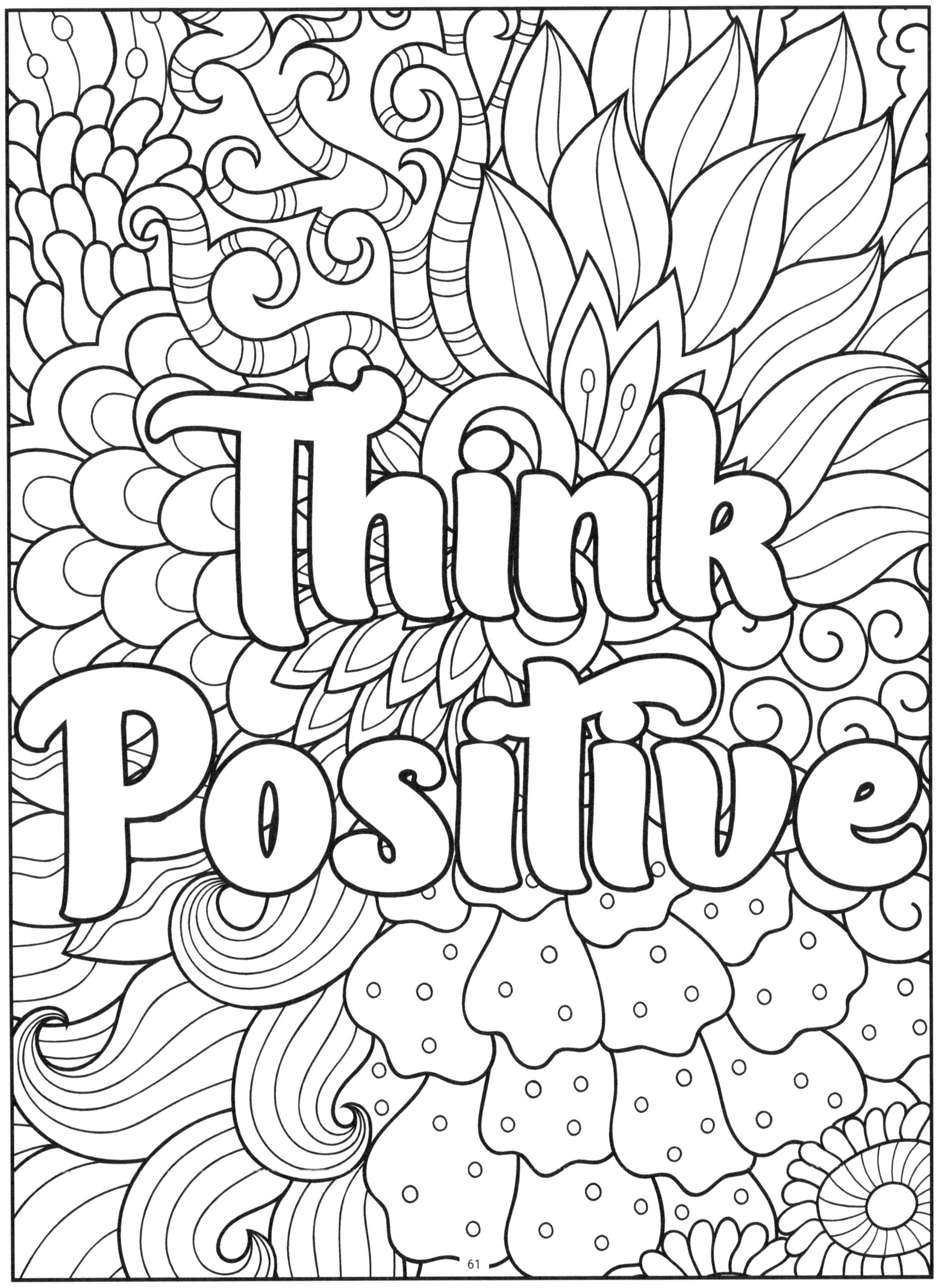

Think
Positive

What Emotions Are Emerging as You Color?

What Symbolism or Significance Do You Attribute to the Colors You've Chose?

Can You Describe the Story or Narrative Behind Your Colorful Picture?

What new things come up from the old memories and experiences?

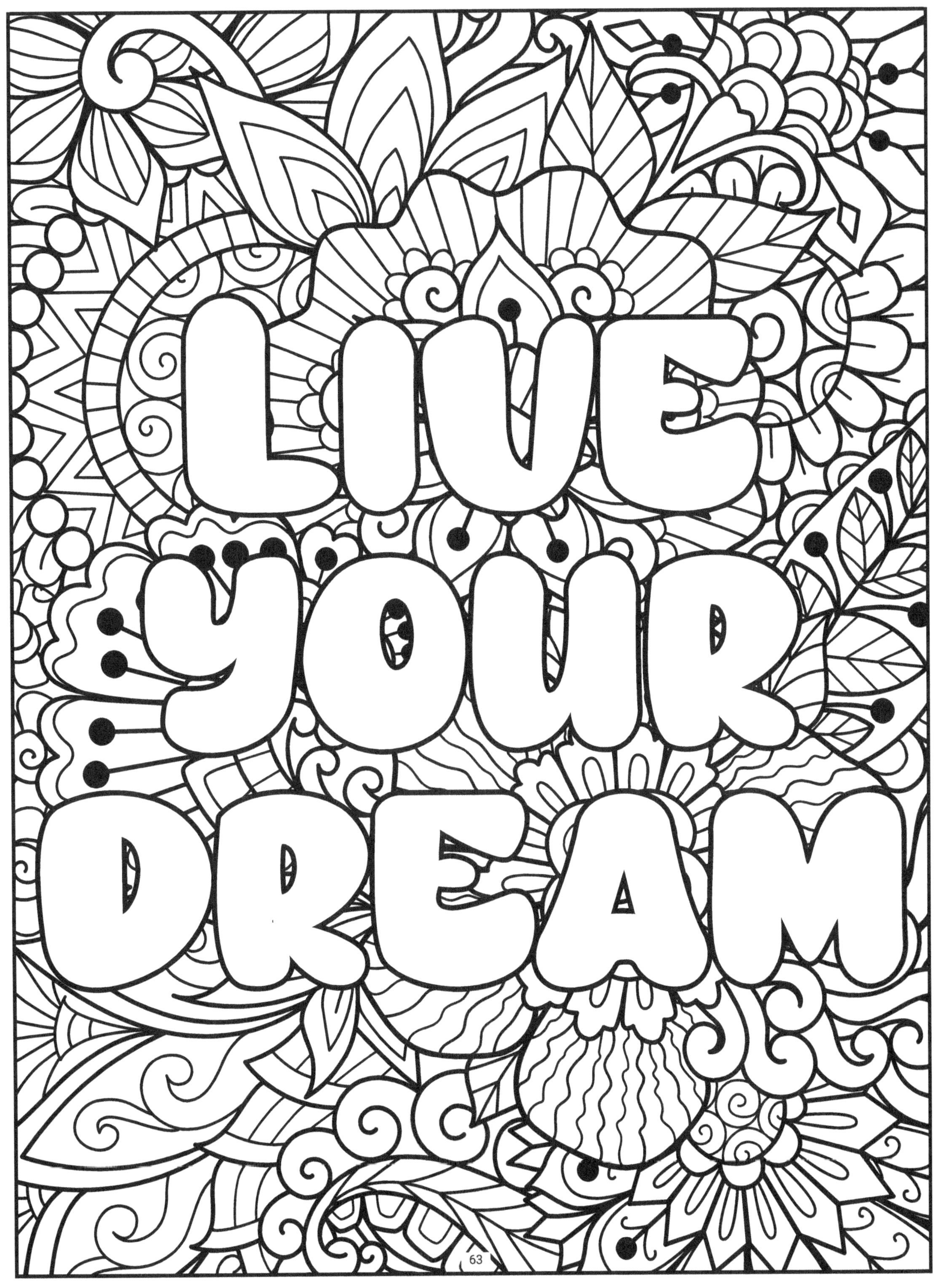

LIVE
YOUR
DREAM

What Emotions Are Emerging as You Color?

What Symbolism or Significance Do You Attribute to the Colors You've Chose?

Can You Describe the Story or Narrative Behind Your Colorful Picture?

What new things come up from the old memories and experiences?

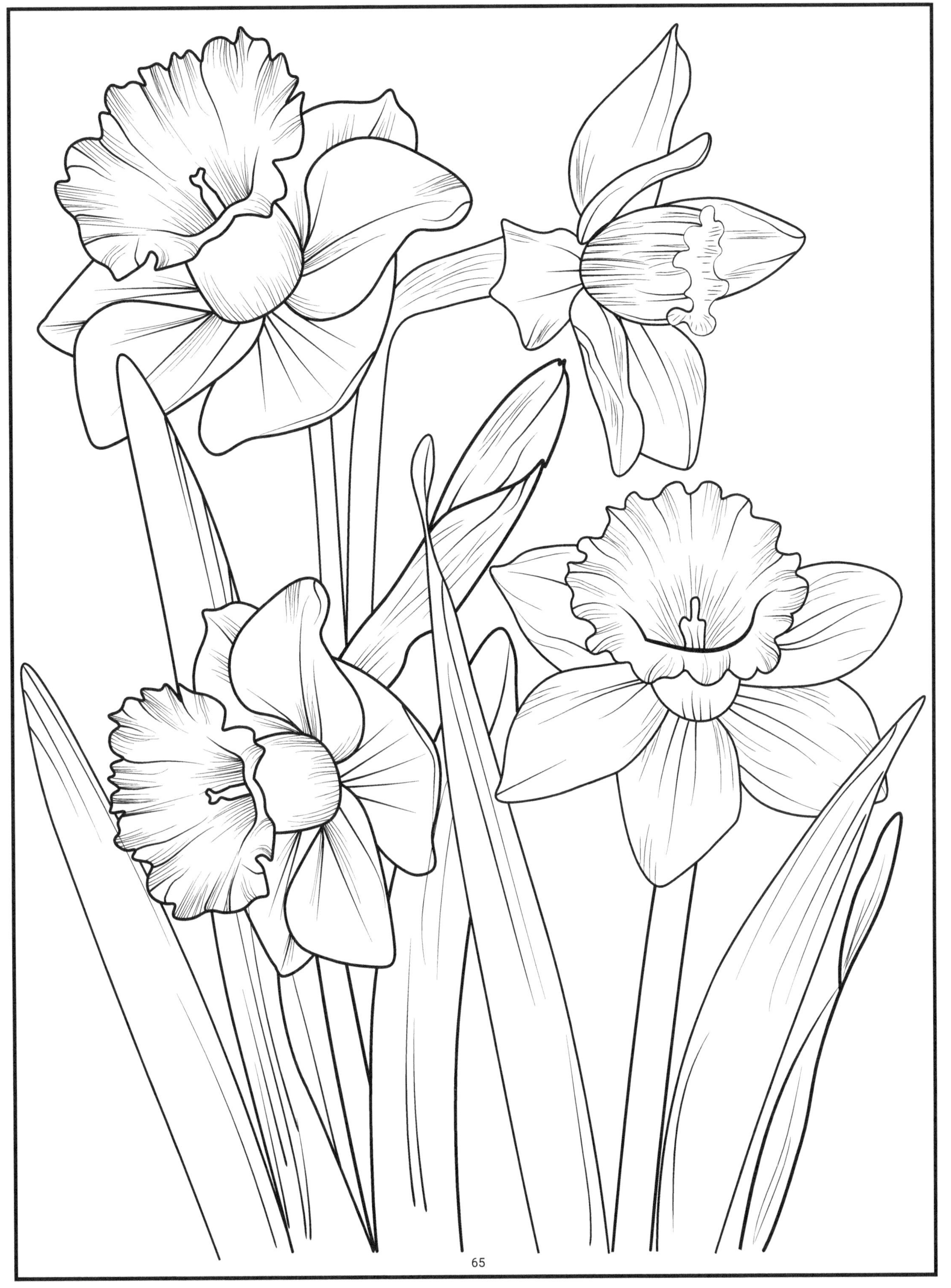

What Emotions Are Emerging as You Color?

What Symbolism or Significance Do You Attribute to the Colors You've Chose?

Can You Describe the Story or Narrative Behind Your Colorful Picture?

What new things come up from the old memories and experiences?

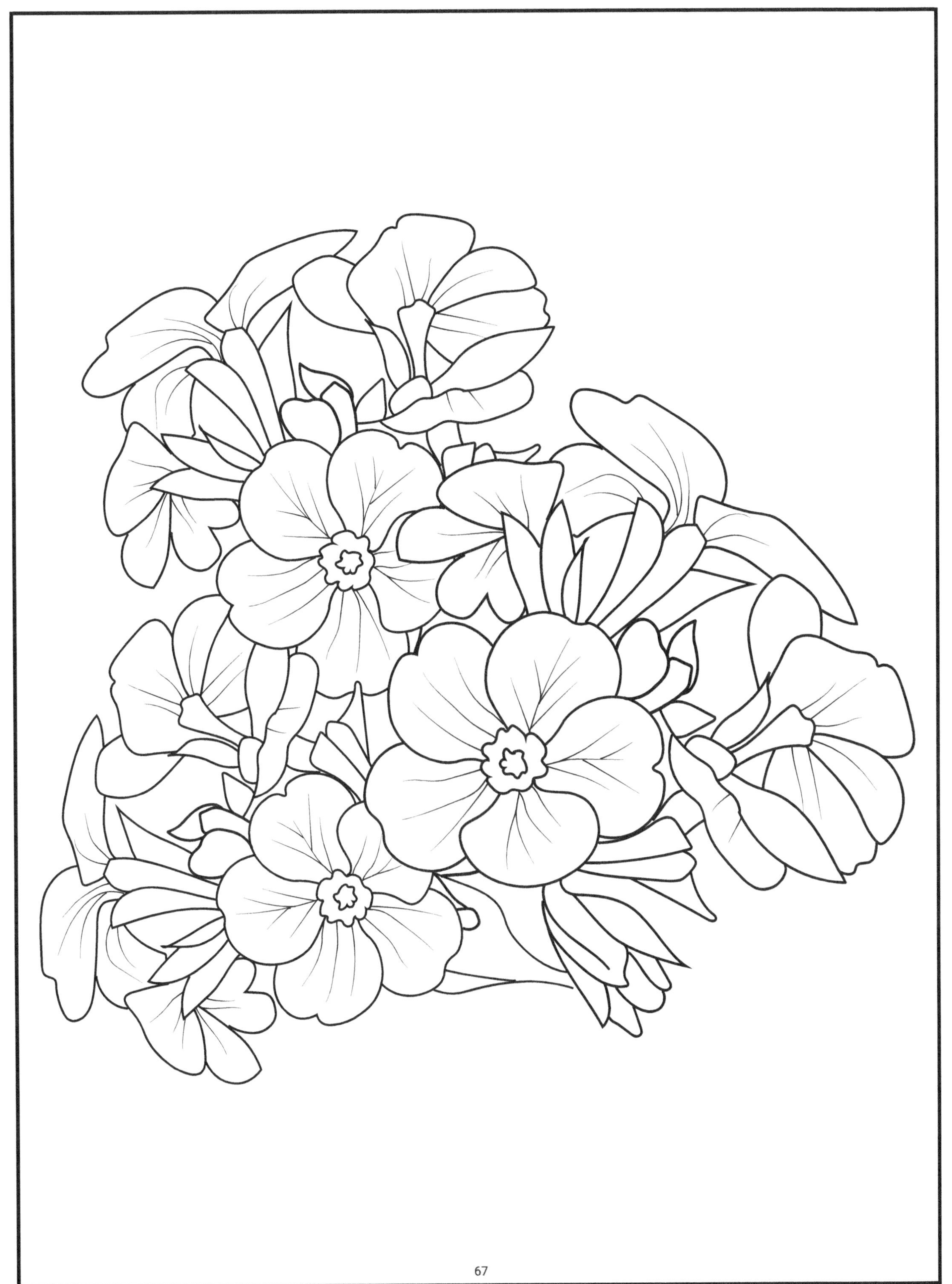

What Emotions Are Emerging as You Color?

What Symbolism or Significance Do You Attribute to the Colors You've Chose?

Can You Describe the Story or Narrative Behind Your Colorful Picture?

What new things come up from the old memories and experiences?

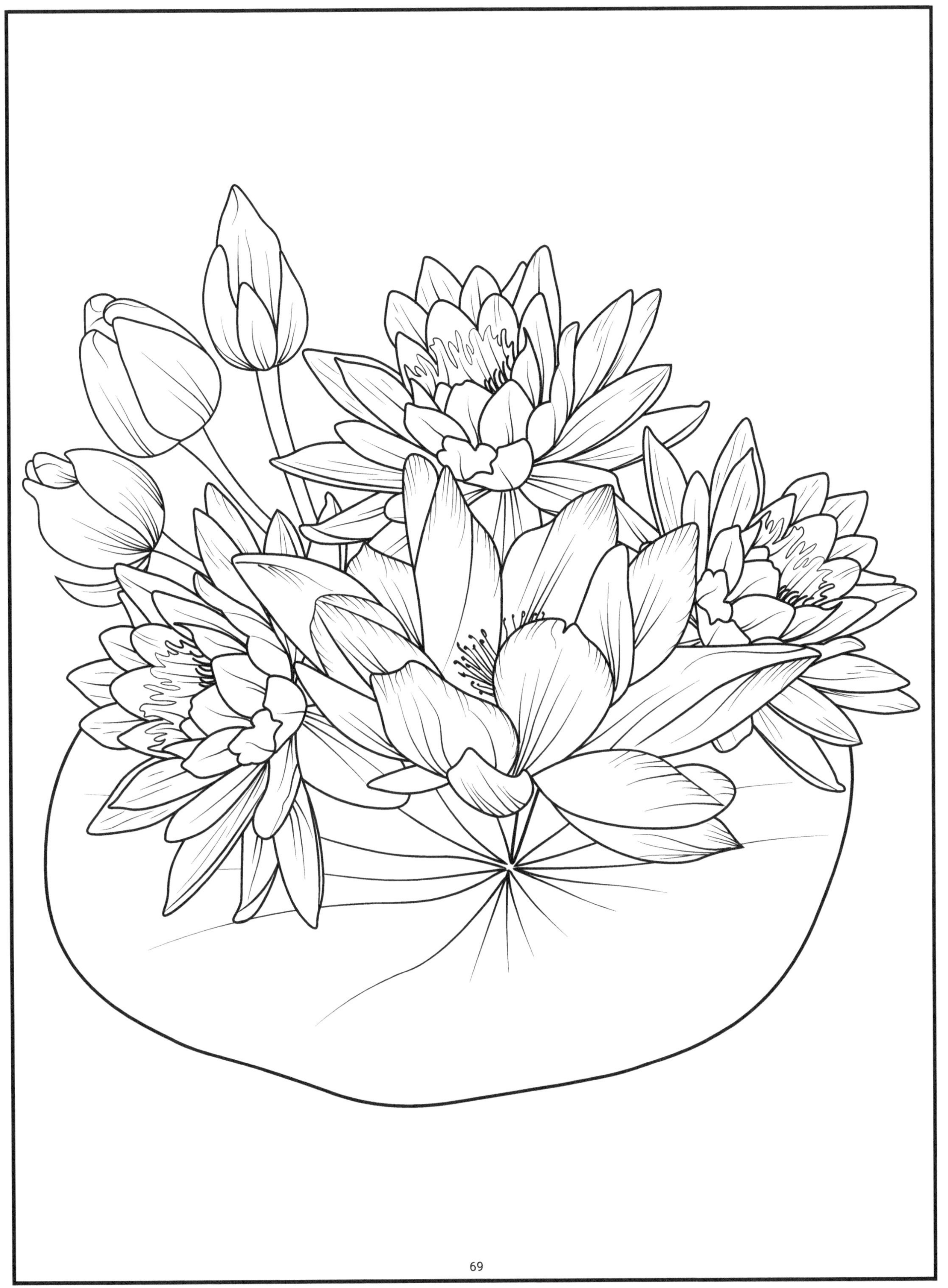

What Emotions Are Emerging as You Color?

What Symbolism or Significance Do You Attribute to the Colors You've Chose?

Can You Describe the Story or Narrative Behind Your Colorful Picture?

What new things come up from the old memories and experiences?

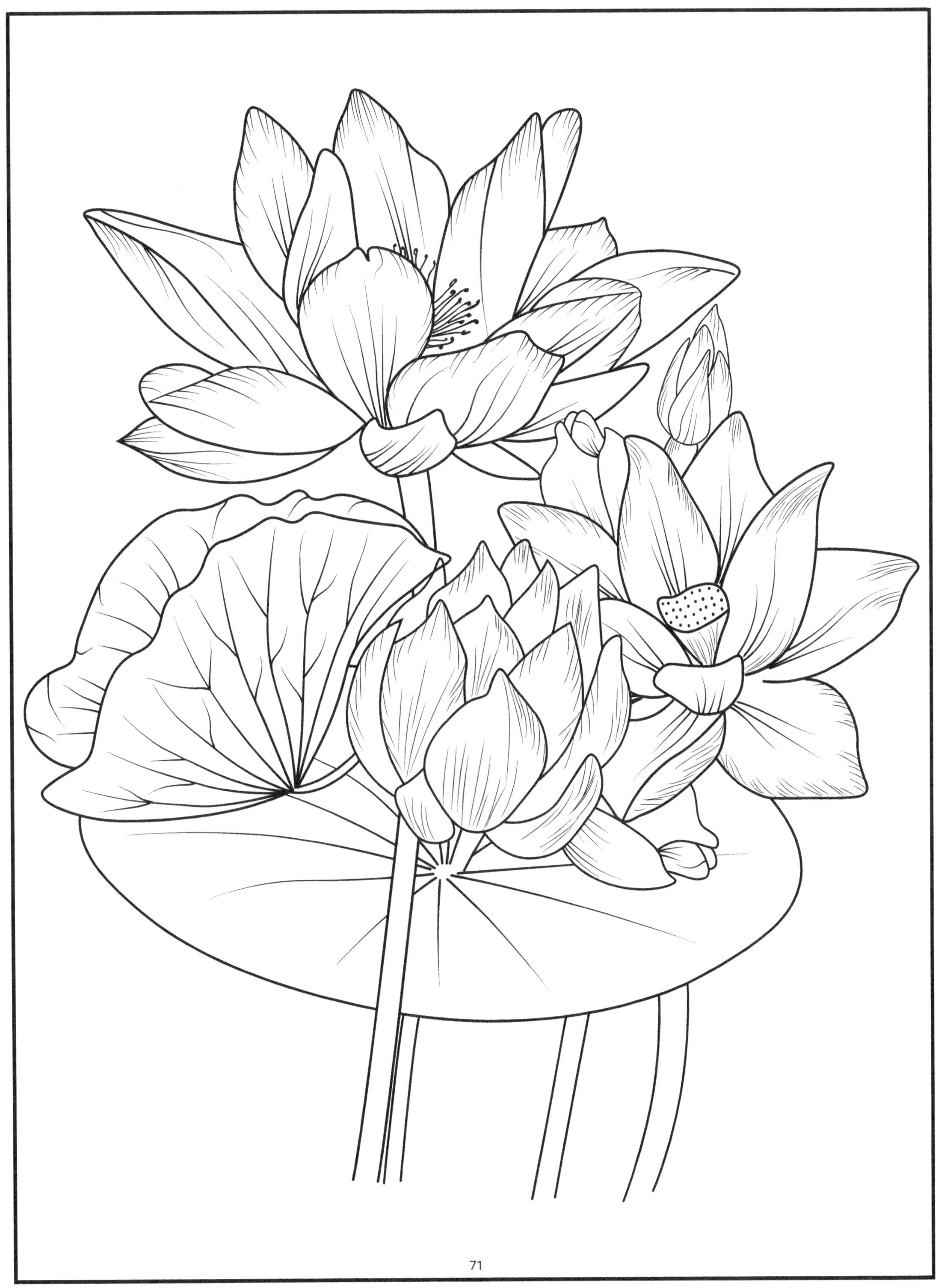

What Emotions Are Emerging as You Color?

What Symbolism or Significance Do You Attribute to the Colors You've Chose?

Can You Describe the Story or Narrative Behind Your Colorful Picture?

What new things come up from the old memories and experiences?

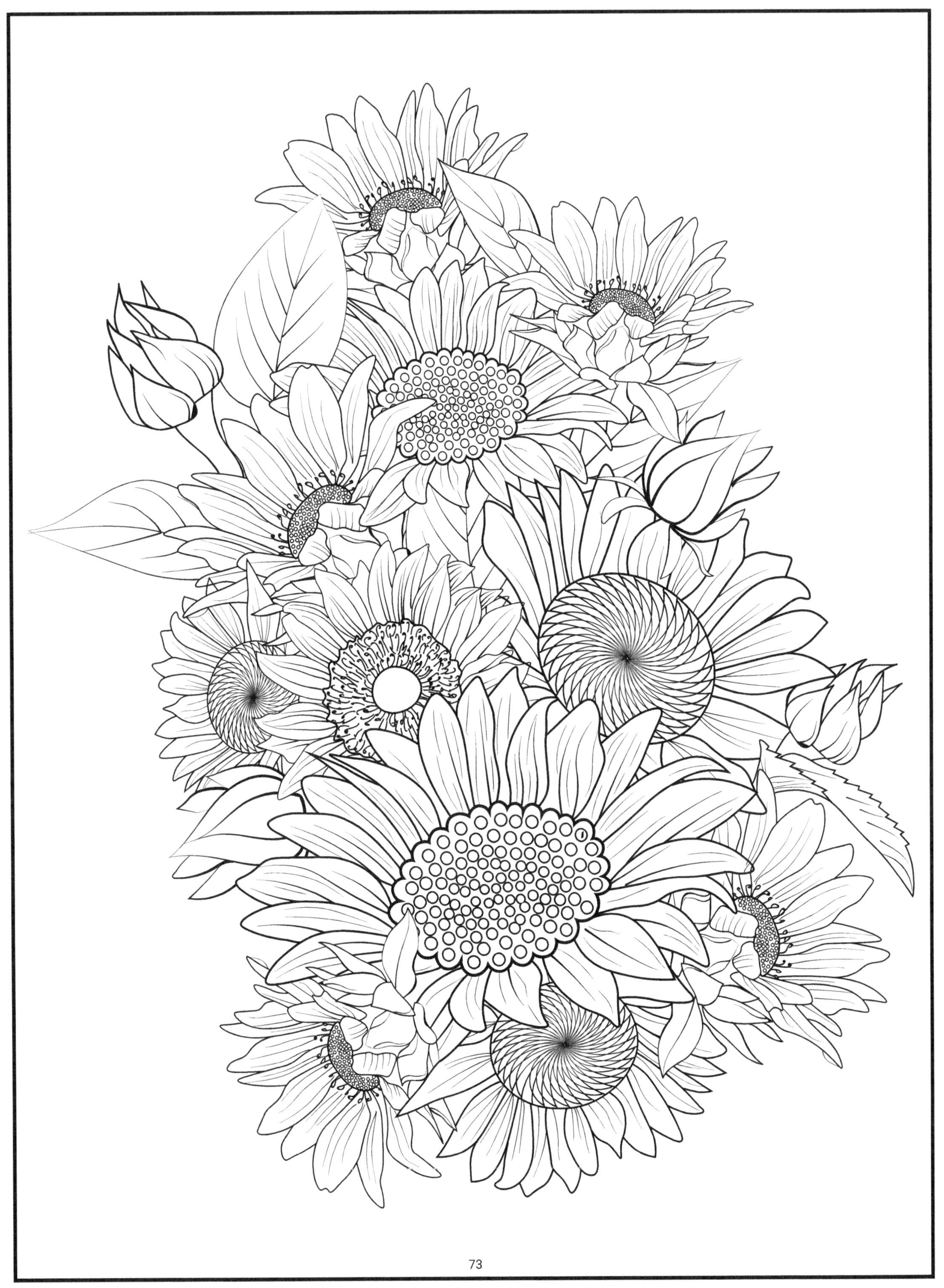

What Emotions Are Emerging as You Color?

What Symbolism or Significance Do You Attribute to the Colors You've Chose?

Can You Describe the Story or Narrative Behind Your Colorful Picture?

What new things come up from the old memories and experiences?

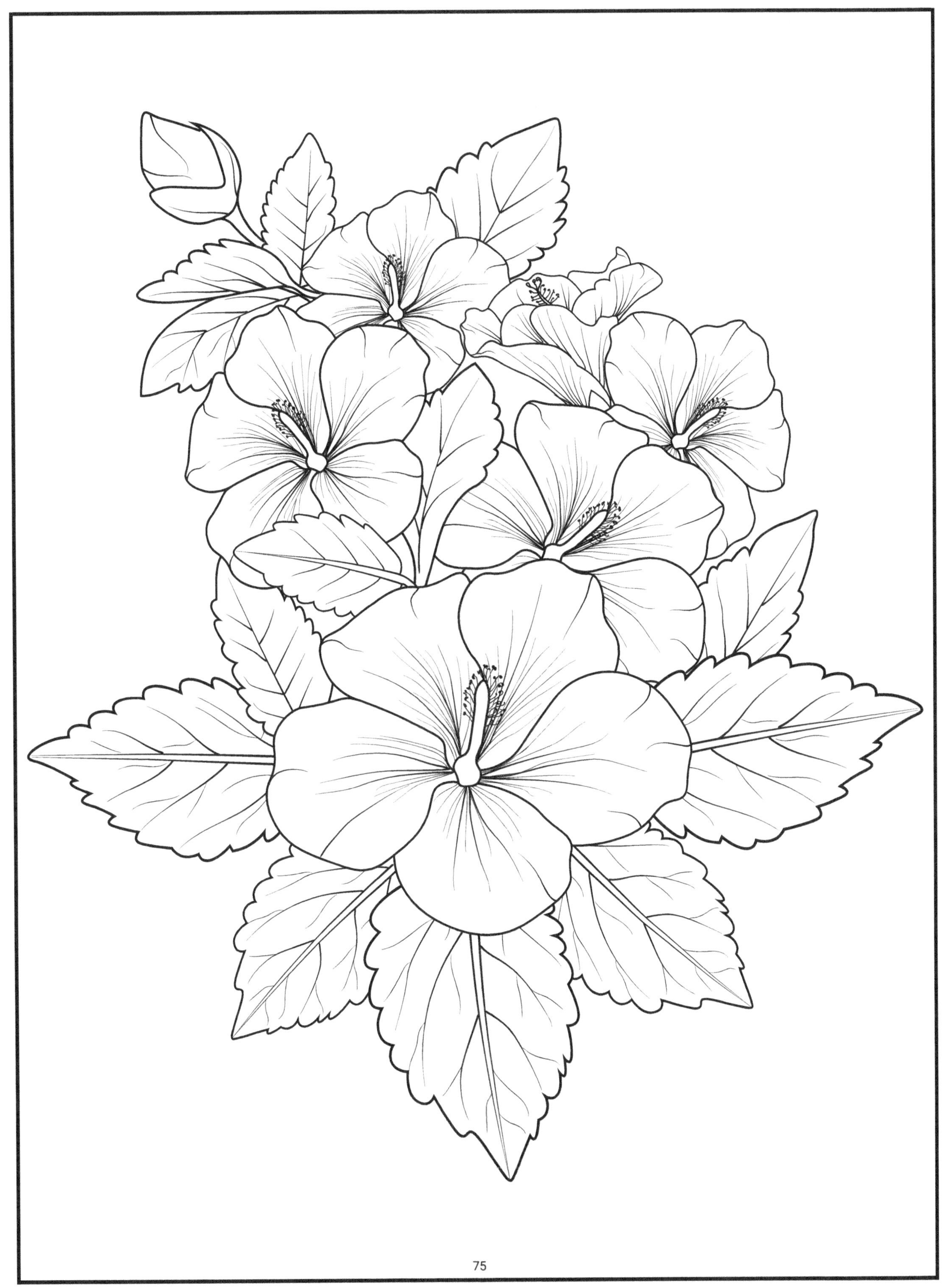

What Emotions Are Emerging as You Color?

What Symbolism or Significance Do You Attribute to the Colors You've Chose?

Can You Describe the Story or Narrative Behind Your Colorful Picture?

What new things come up from the old memories and experiences?

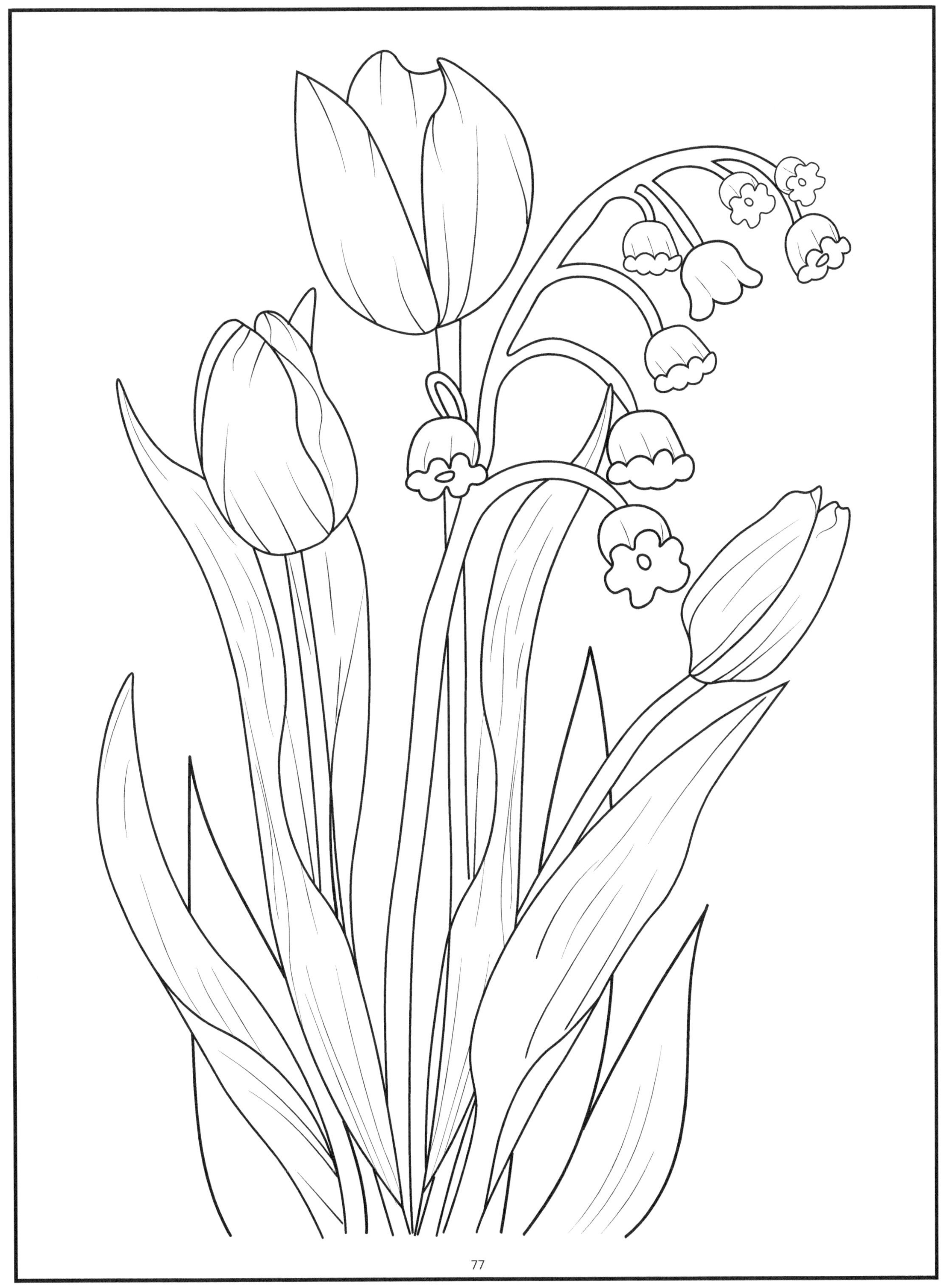

What Emotions Are Emerging as You Color?

What Symbolism or Significance Do You Attribute to the Colors You've Chose?

Can You Describe the Story or Narrative Behind Your Colorful Picture?

What new things come up from the old memories and experiences?

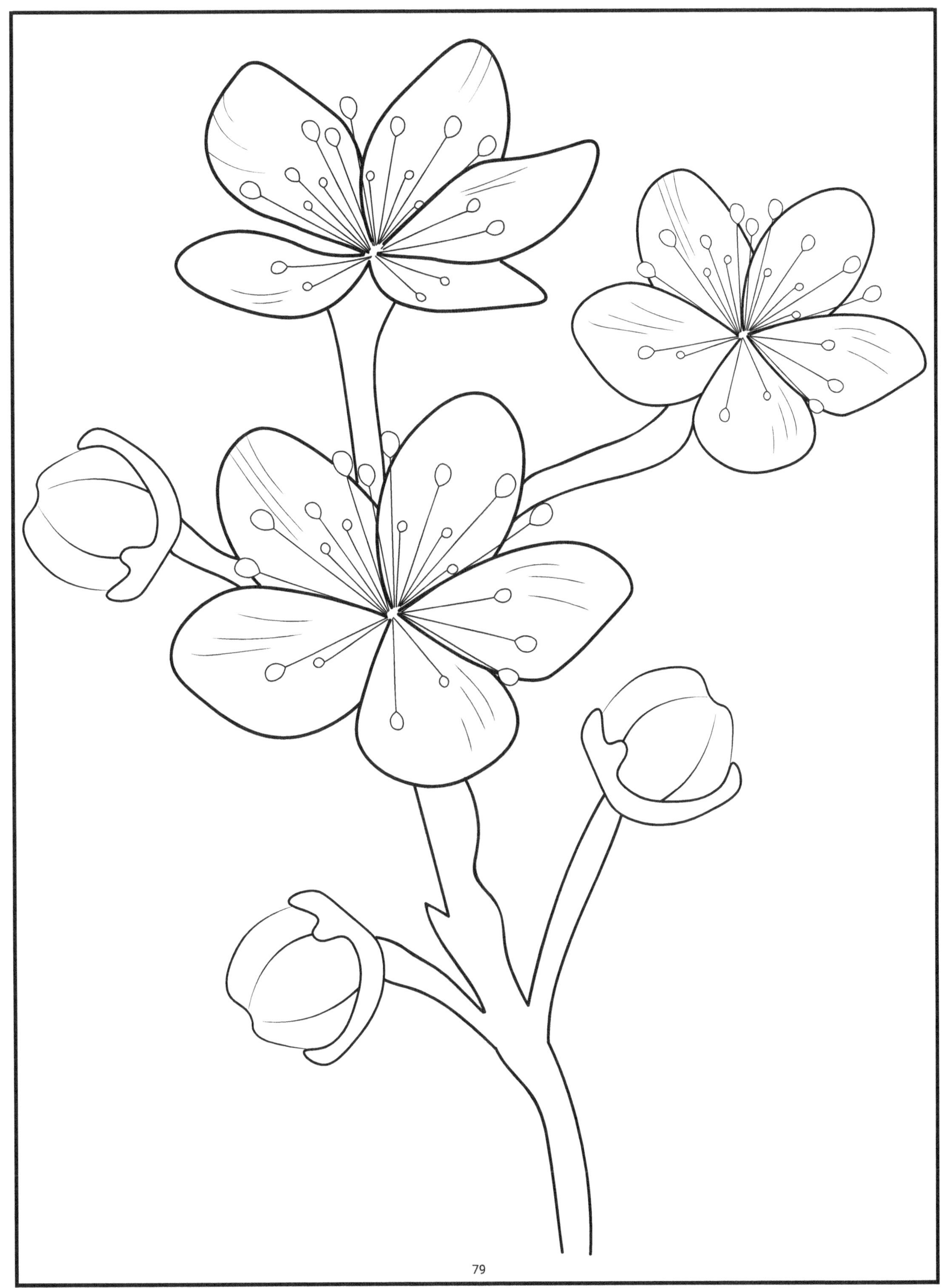

What Emotions Are Emerging as You Color?

What Symbolism or Significance Do You Attribute to the Colors You've Chose?

Can You Describe the Story or Narrative Behind Your Colorful Picture?

What new things come up from the old memories and experiences?

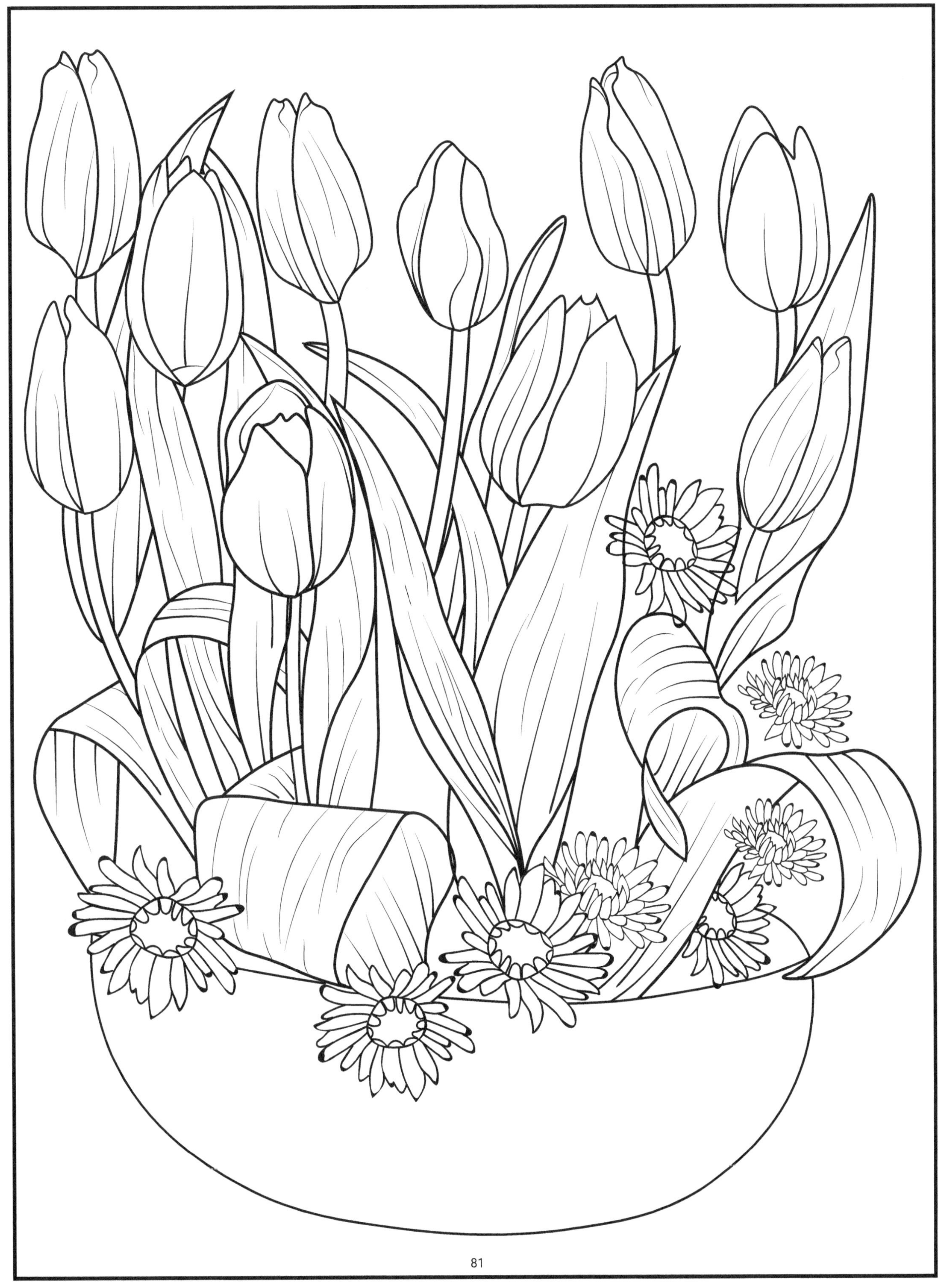

What Emotions Are Emerging as You Color?

What Symbolism or Significance Do You Attribute to the Colors You've Chose?

Can You Describe the Story or Narrative Behind Your Colorful Picture?

What new things come up from the old memories and experiences?

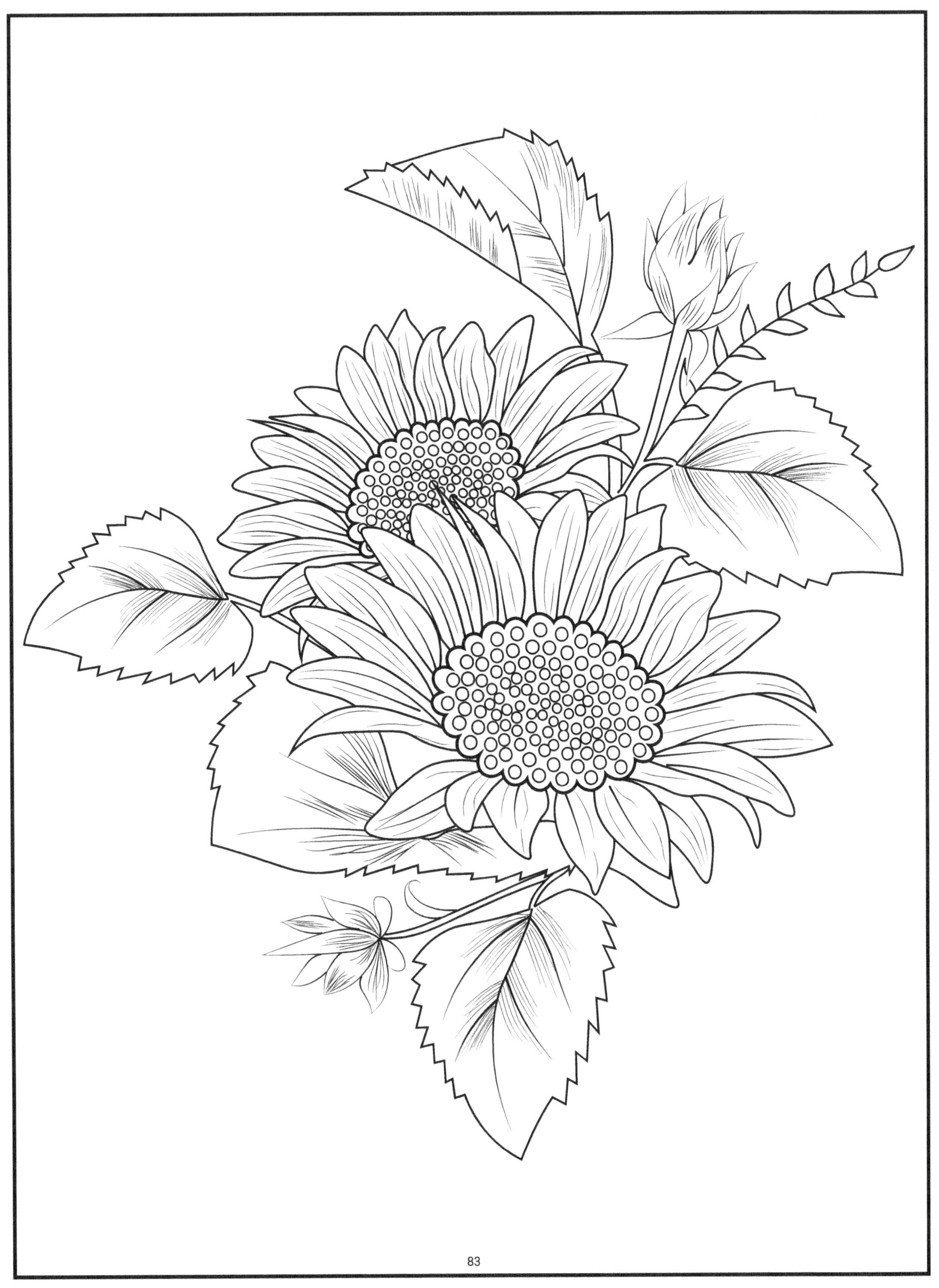

What Emotions Are Emerging as You Color?

What Symbolism or Significance Do You Attribute to the Colors You've Chose?

Can You Describe the Story or Narrative Behind Your Colorful Picture?

What new things come up from the old memories and experiences?

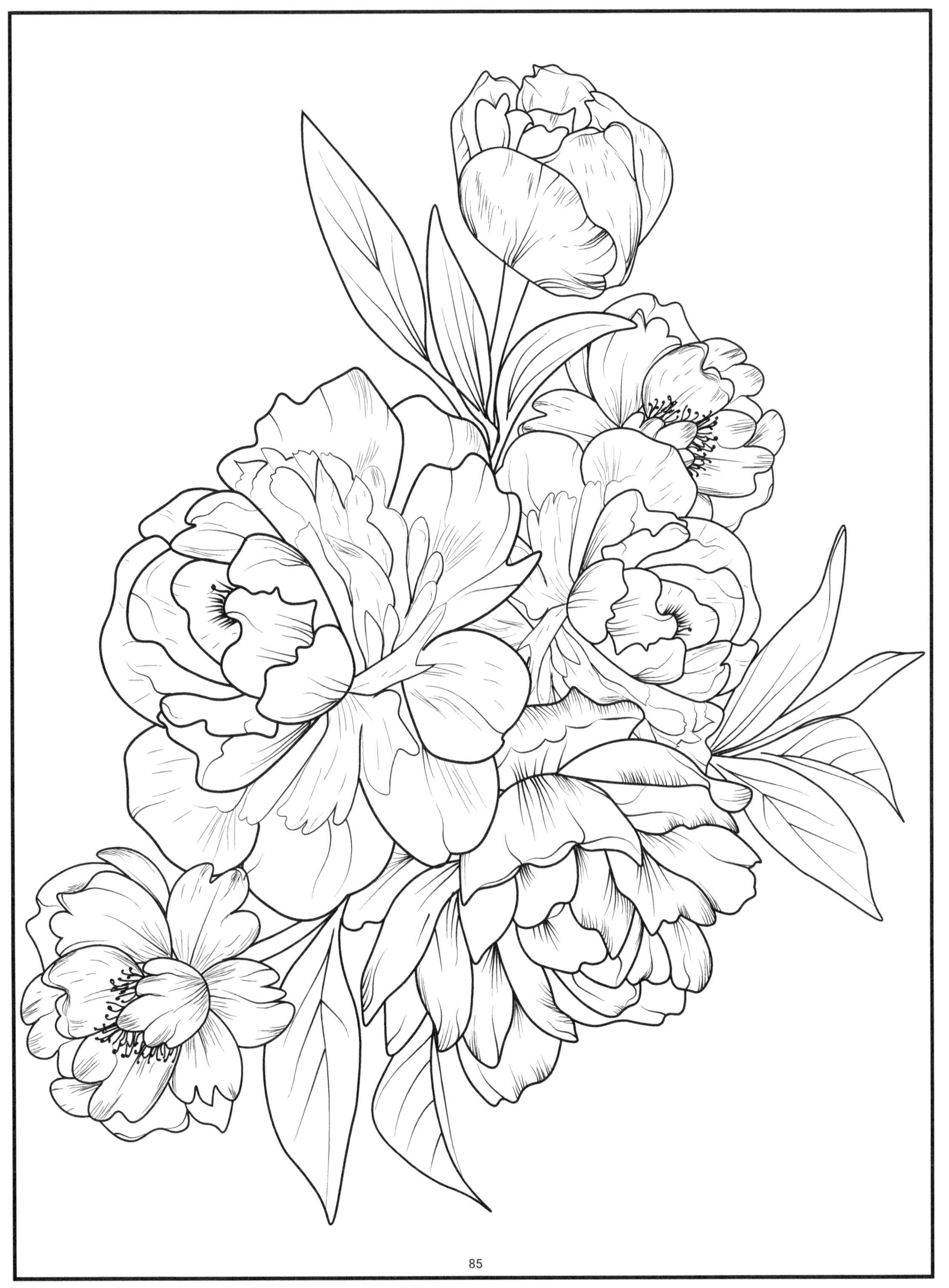

What Emotions Are Emerging as You Color?

What Symbolism or Significance Do You Attribute to the Colors You've Chose?

Can You Describe the Story or Narrative Behind Your Colorful Picture?

What new things come up from the old memories and experiences?

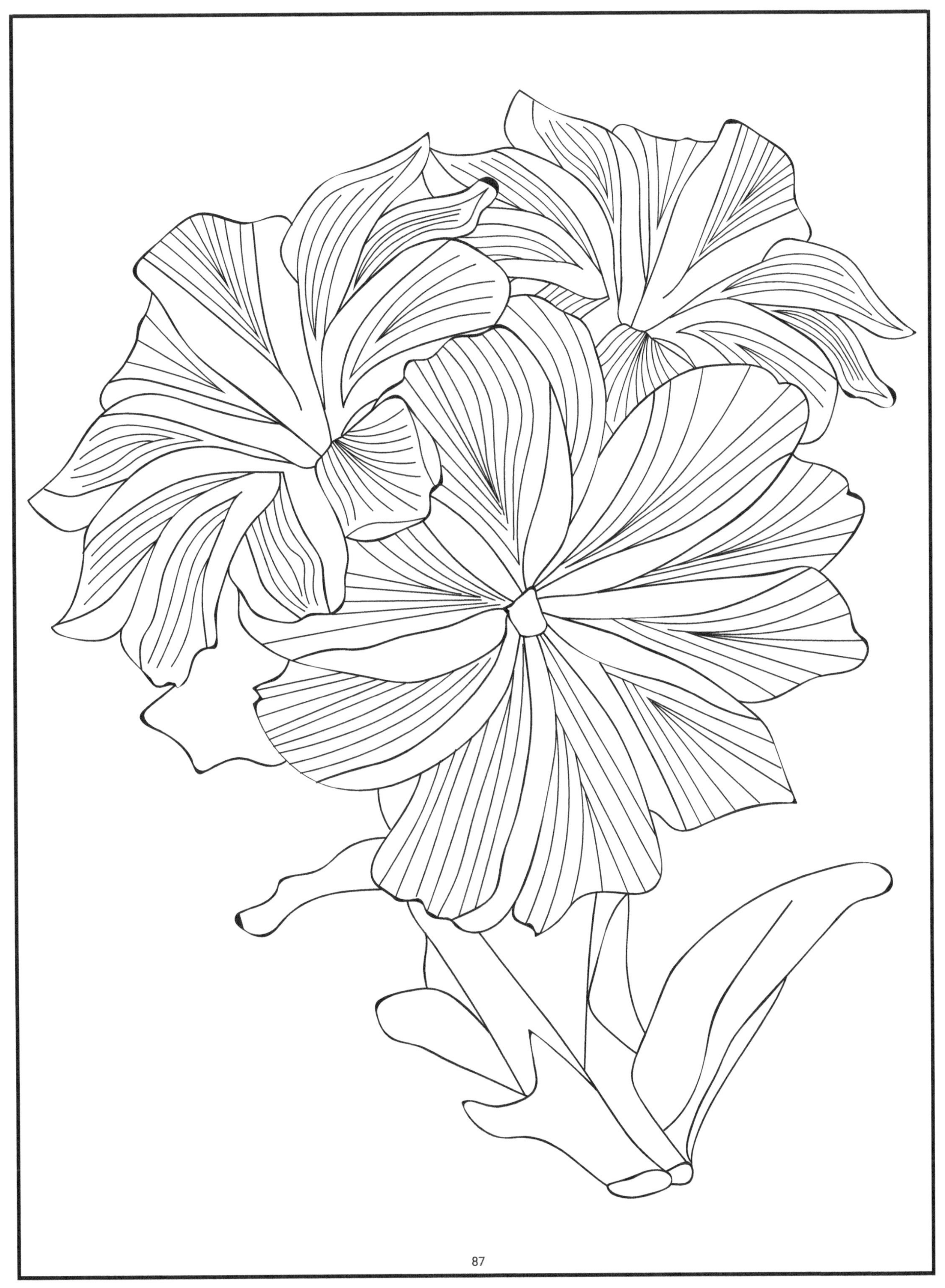

What Emotions Are Emerging as You Color?

What Symbolism or Significance Do You Attribute to the Colors You've Chose?

Can You Describe the Story or Narrative Behind Your Colorful Picture?

What new things come up from the old memories and experiences?

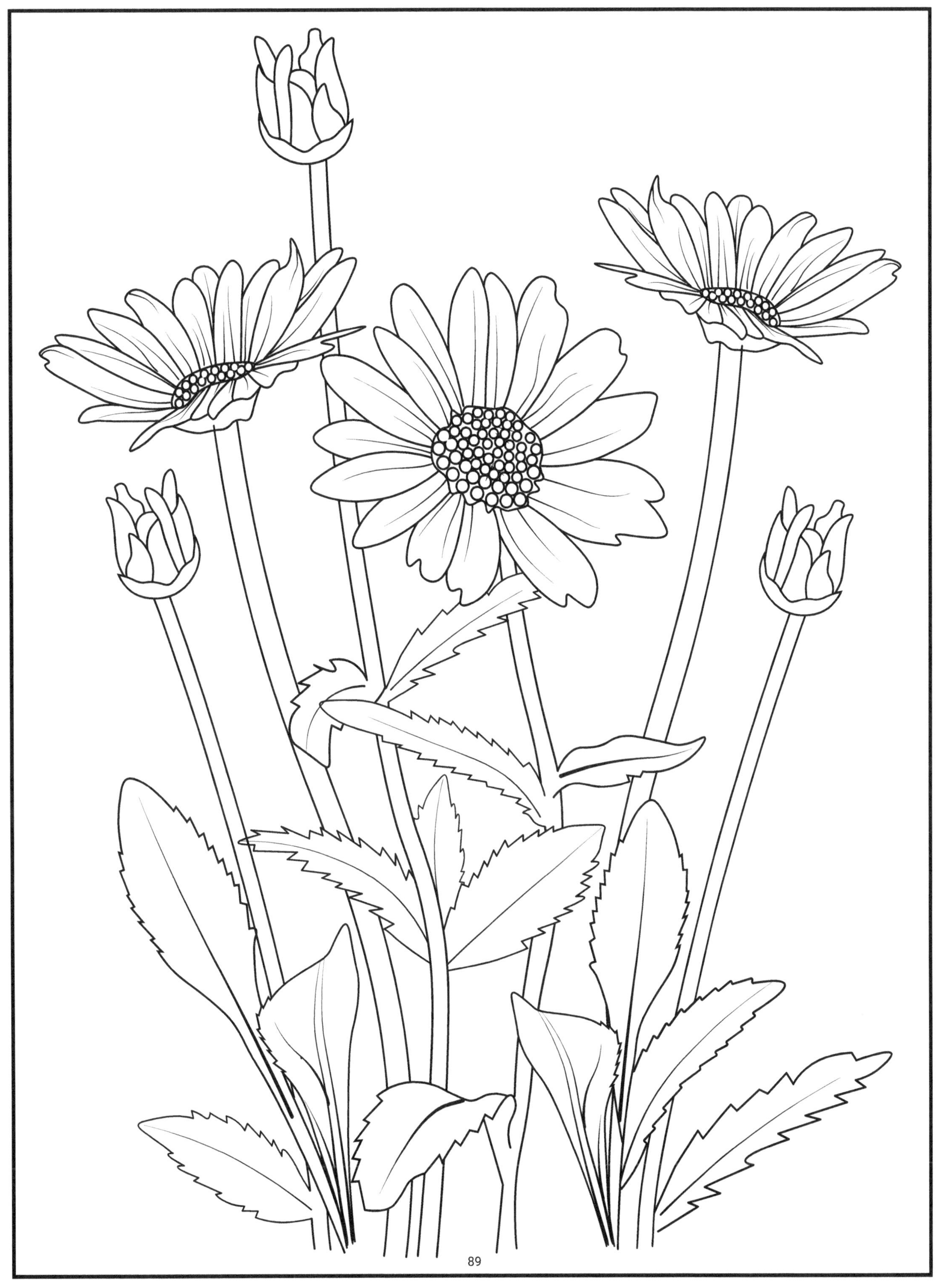

What Emotions Are Emerging as You Color?

What Symbolism or Significance Do You Attribute to the Colors You've Chose?

Can You Describe the Story or Narrative Behind Your Colorful Picture?

What new things come up from the old memories and experiences?

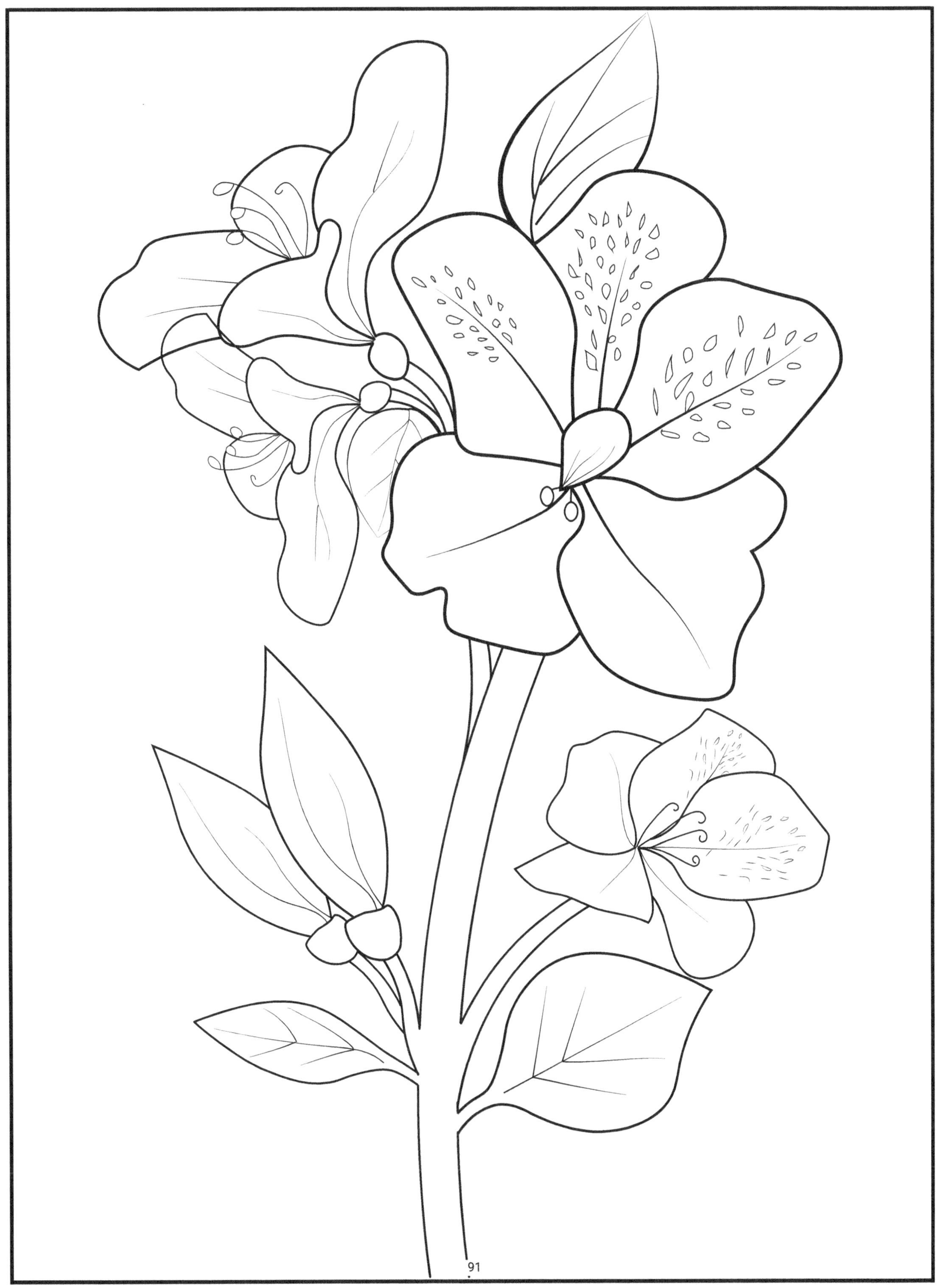

What Emotions Are Emerging as You Color?

What Symbolism or Significance Do You Attribute to the Colors You've Chose?

Can You Describe the Story or Narrative Behind Your Colorful Picture?

What new things come up from the old memories and experiences?

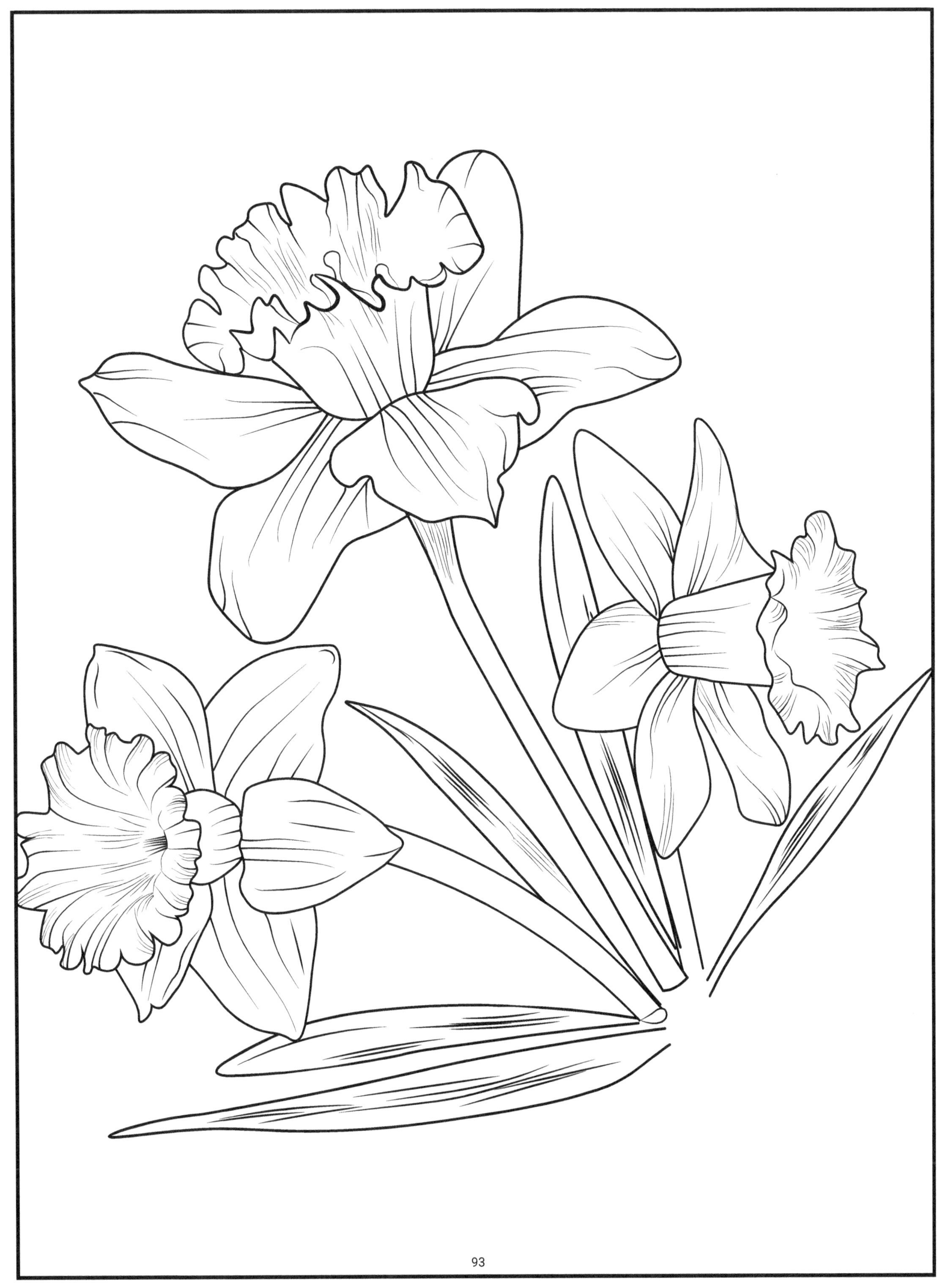

What Emotions Are Emerging as You Color?

What Symbolism or Significance Do You Attribute to the Colors You've Chose?

Can You Describe the Story or Narrative Behind Your Colorful Picture?

What new things come up from the old memories and experiences?

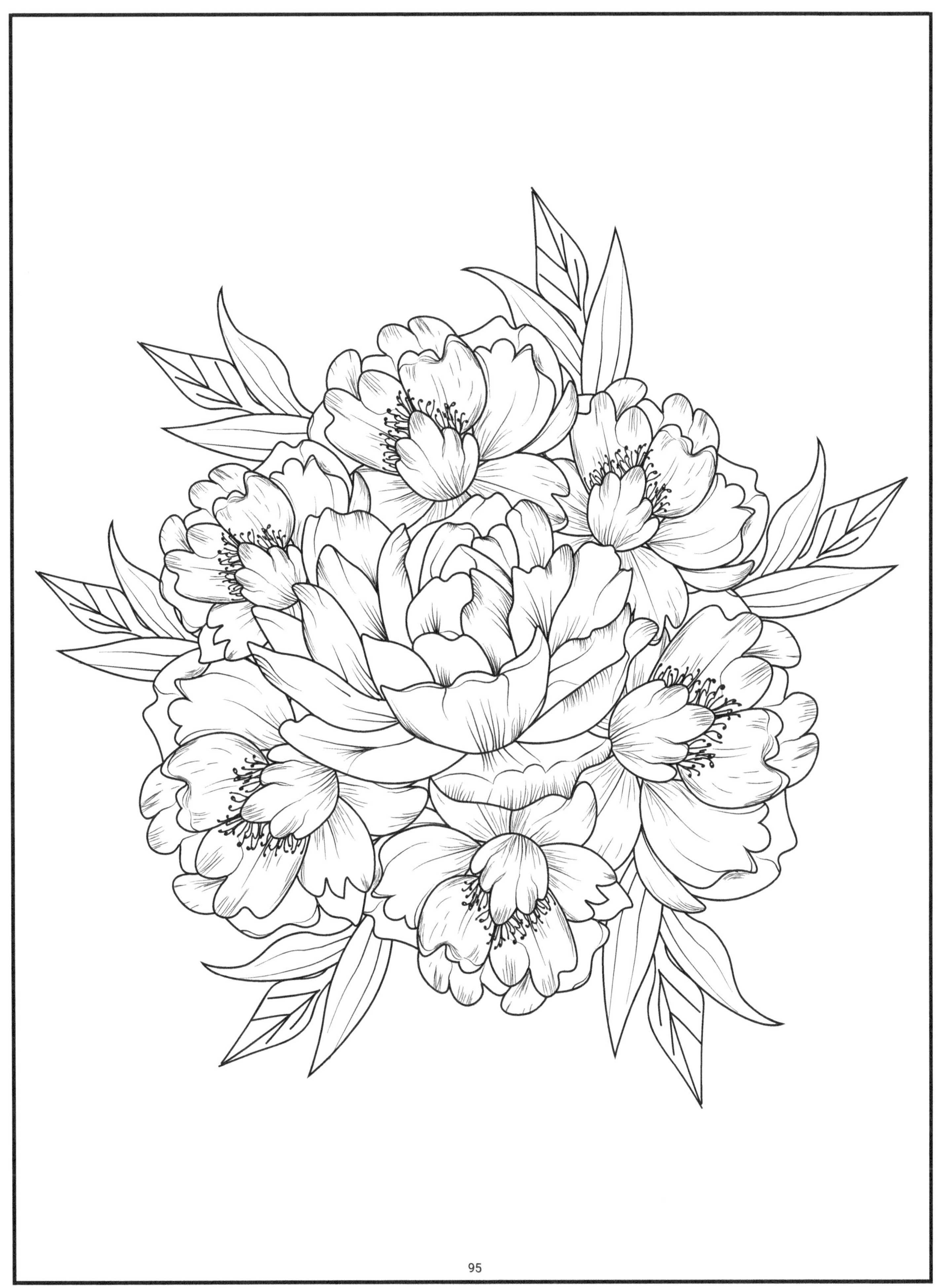

What Emotions Are Emerging as You Color?

What Symbolism or Significance Do You Attribute to the Colors You've Chose?

Can You Describe the Story or Narrative Behind Your Colorful Picture?

What new things come up from the old memories and experiences?

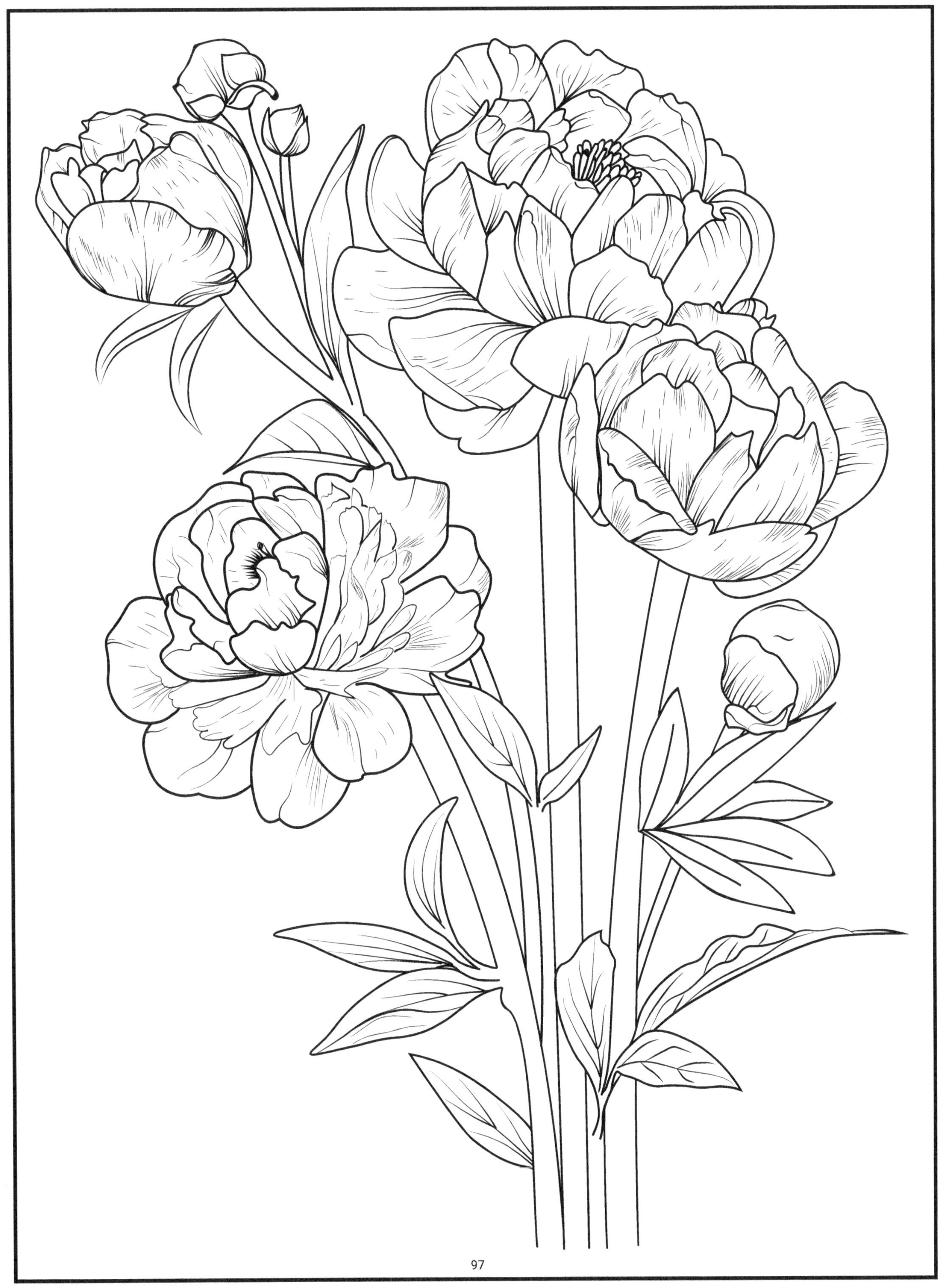

What Emotions Are Emerging as You Color?

What Symbolism or Significance Do You Attribute to the Colors You've Chose?

Can You Describe the Story or Narrative Behind Your Colorful Picture?

What new things come up from the old memories and experiences?

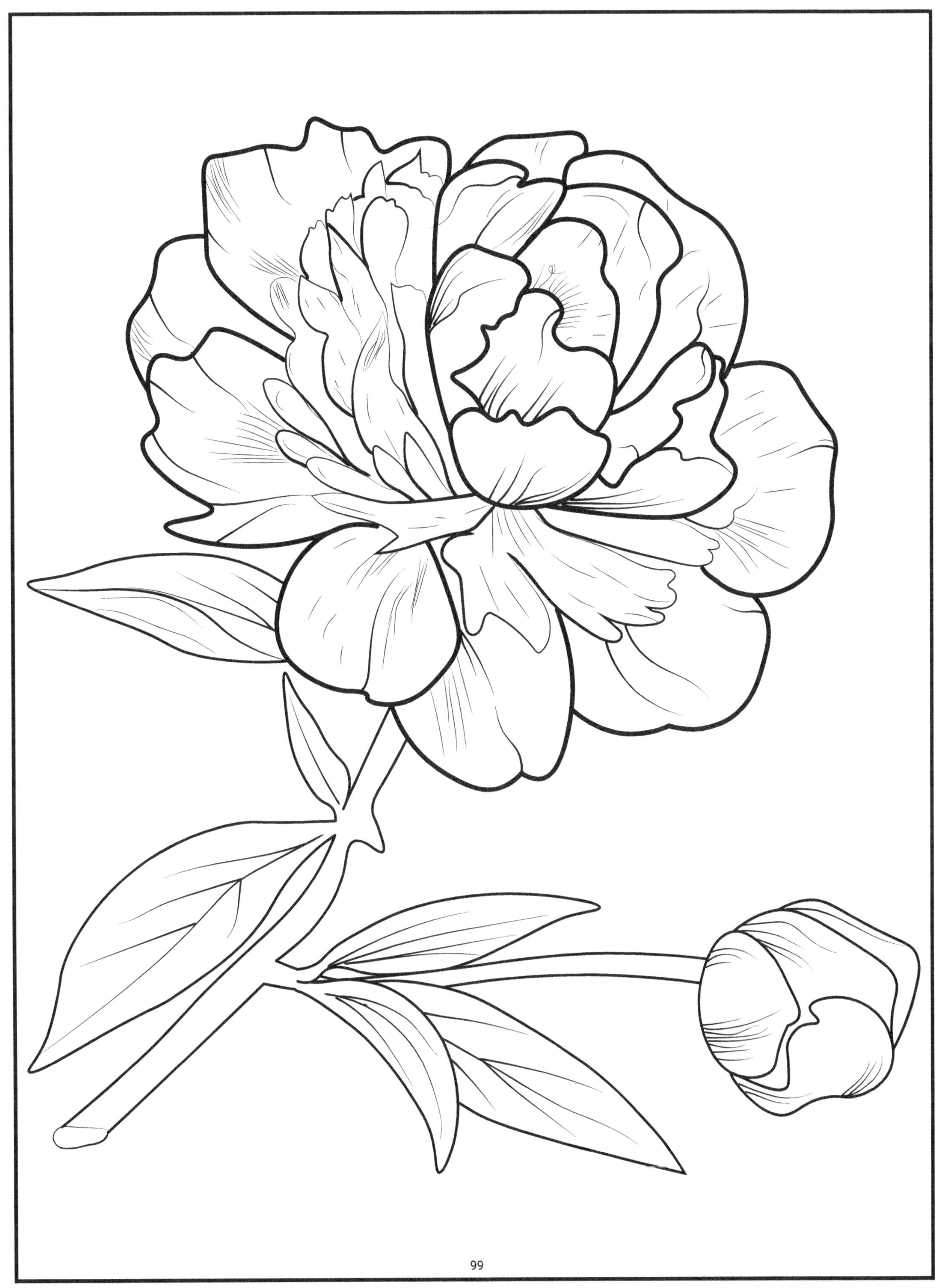

What Emotions Are Emerging as You Color?

What Symbolism or Significance Do You Attribute to the Colors You've Chose?

Can You Describe the Story or Narrative Behind Your Colorful Picture?

What new things come up from the old memories and experiences?

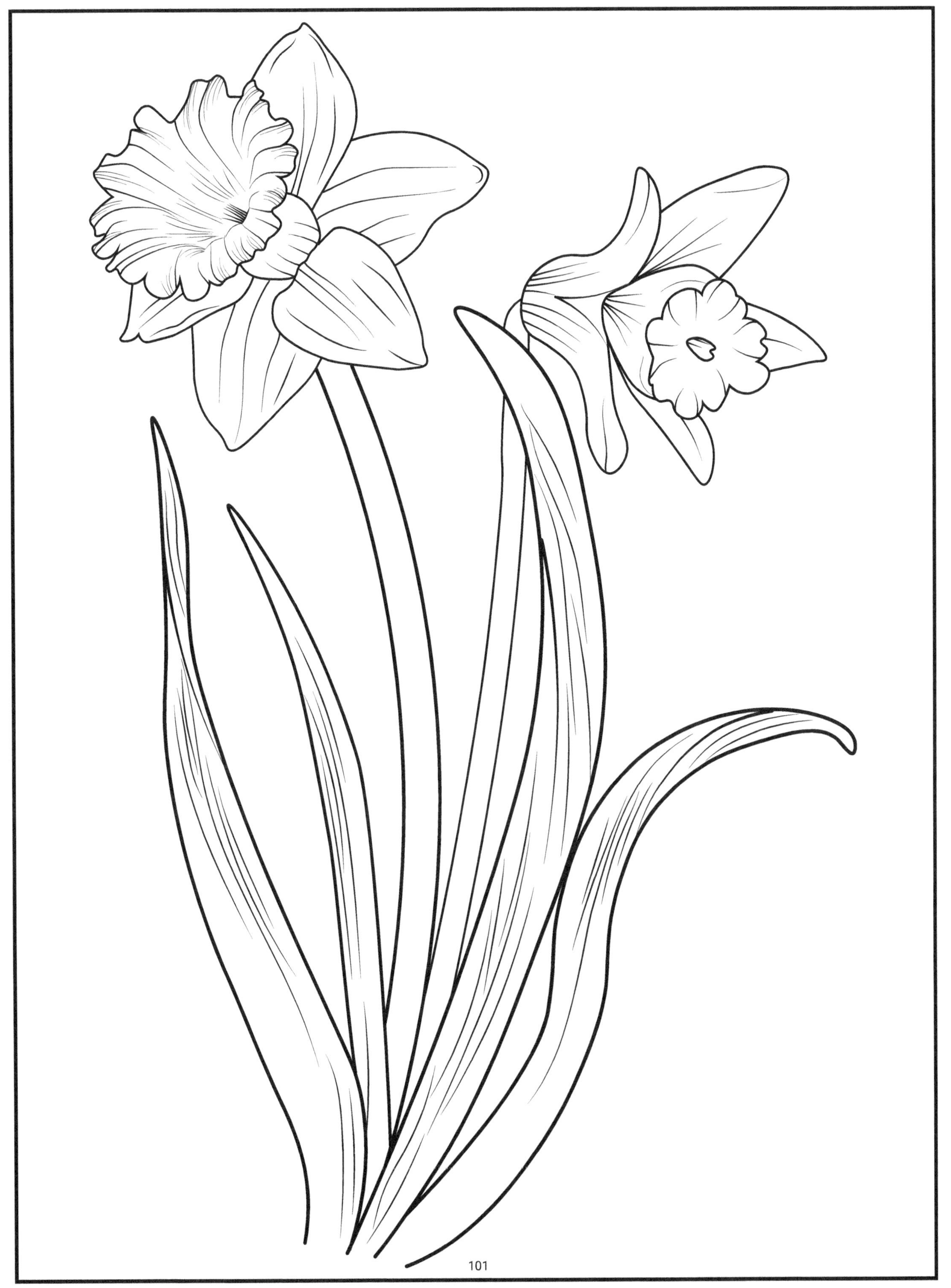

What Emotions Are Emerging as You Color?

What Symbolism or Significance Do You Attribute to the Colors You've Chose?

Can You Describe the Story or Narrative Behind Your Colorful Picture?

What new things come up from the old memories and experiences?

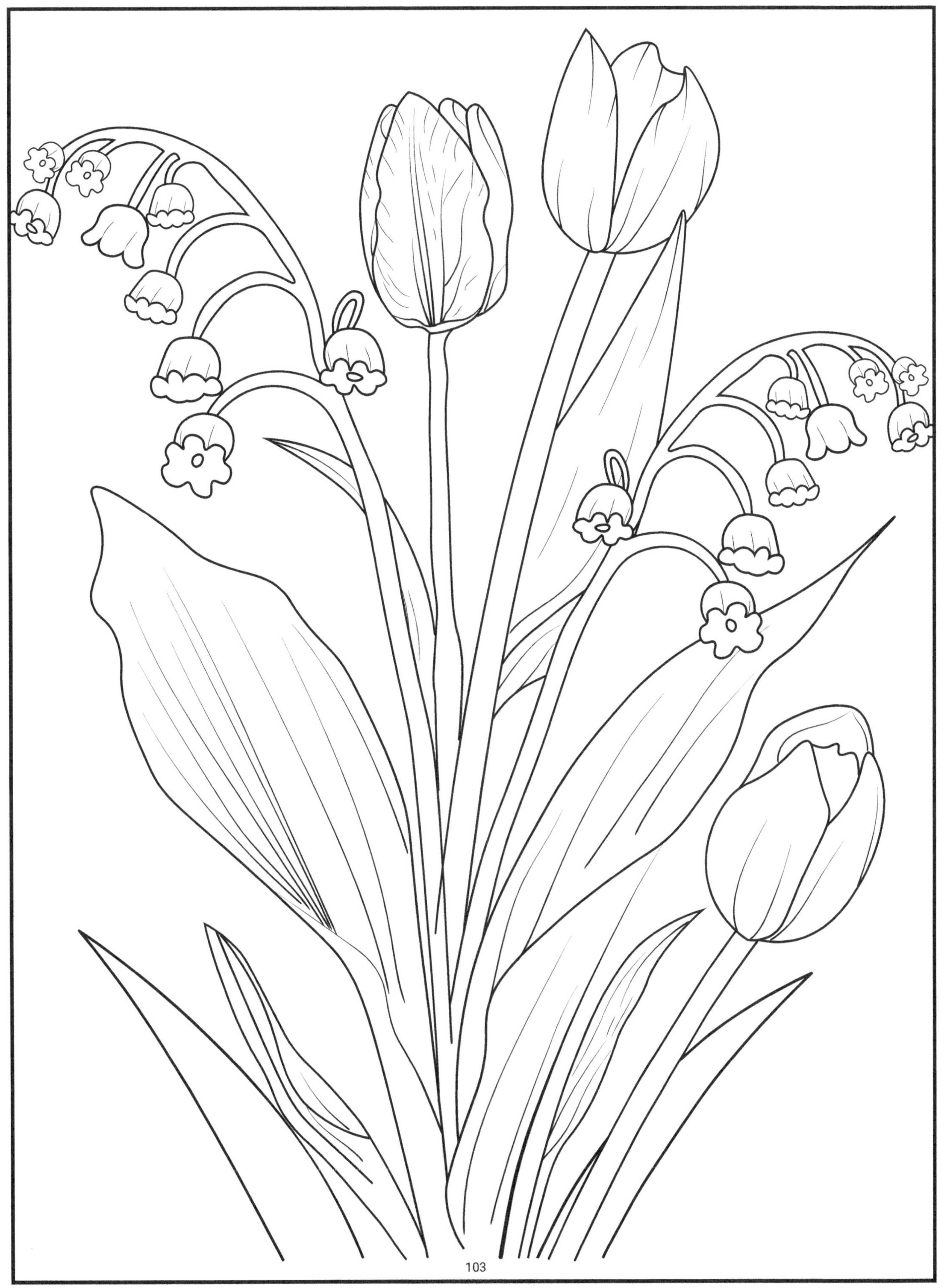

What Emotions Are Emerging as You Color?

What Symbolism or Significance Do You Attribute to the Colors You've Chose?

Can You Describe the Story or Narrative Behind Your Colorful Picture?

What new things come up from the old memories and experiences?

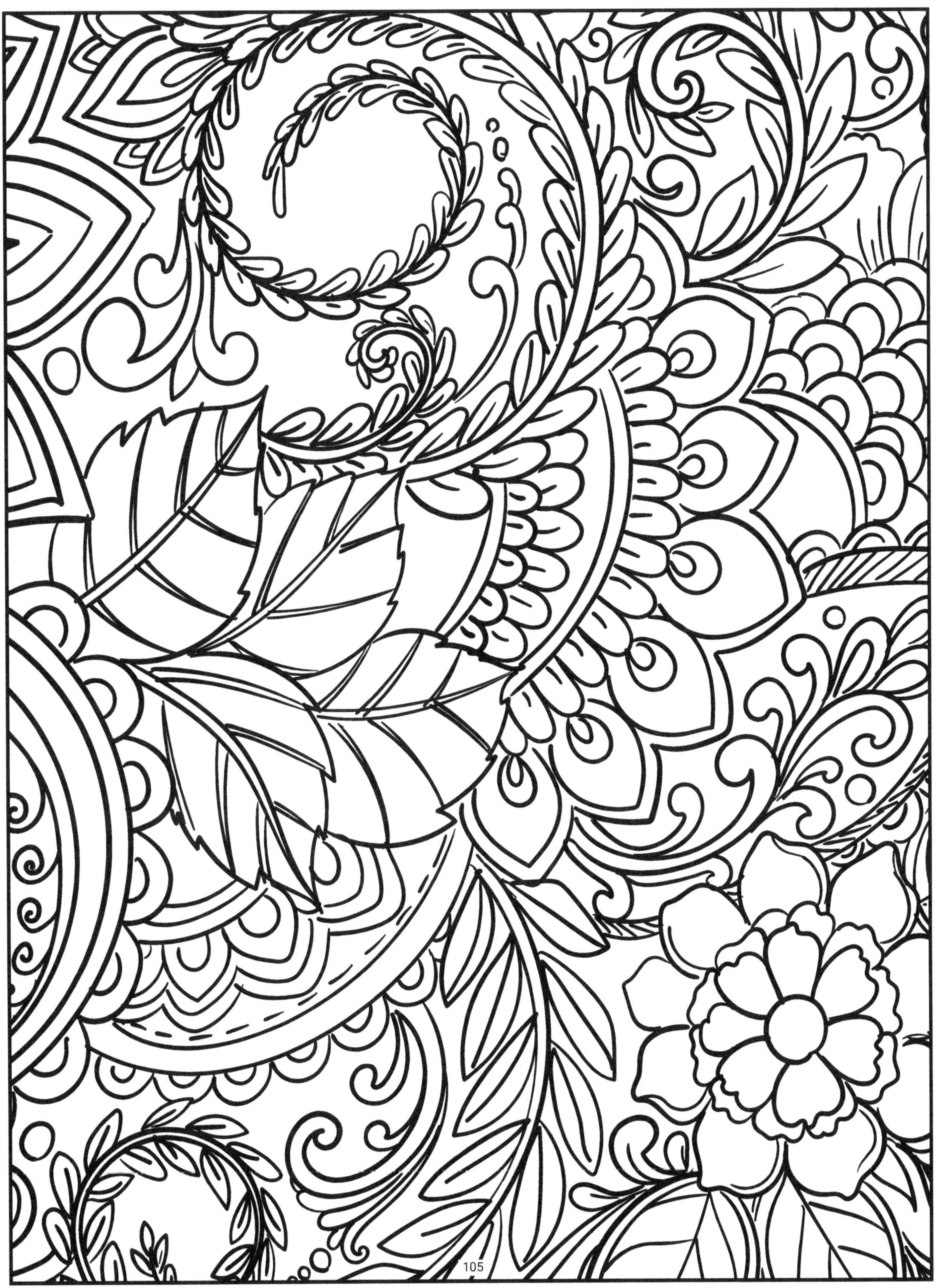

What Emotions Are Emerging as You Color?

What Symbolism or Significance Do You Attribute to the Colors You've Chose?

Can You Describe the Story or Narrative Behind Your Colorful Picture?

What new things come up from the old memories and experiences?

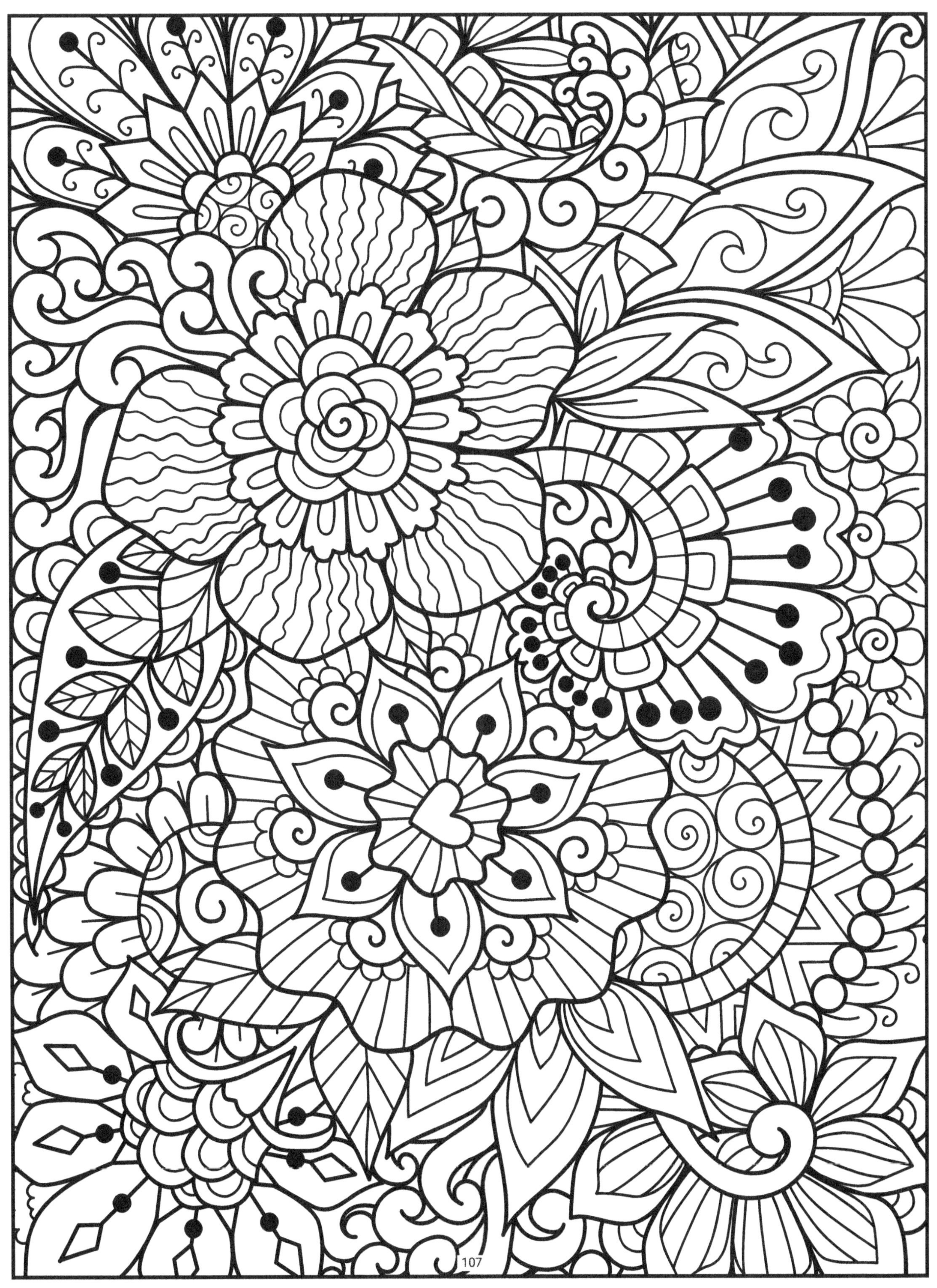

What Emotions Are Emerging as You Color?

What Symbolism or Significance Do You Attribute to the Colors You've Chose?

Can You Describe the Story or Narrative Behind Your Colorful Picture?

What new things come up from the old memories and experiences?

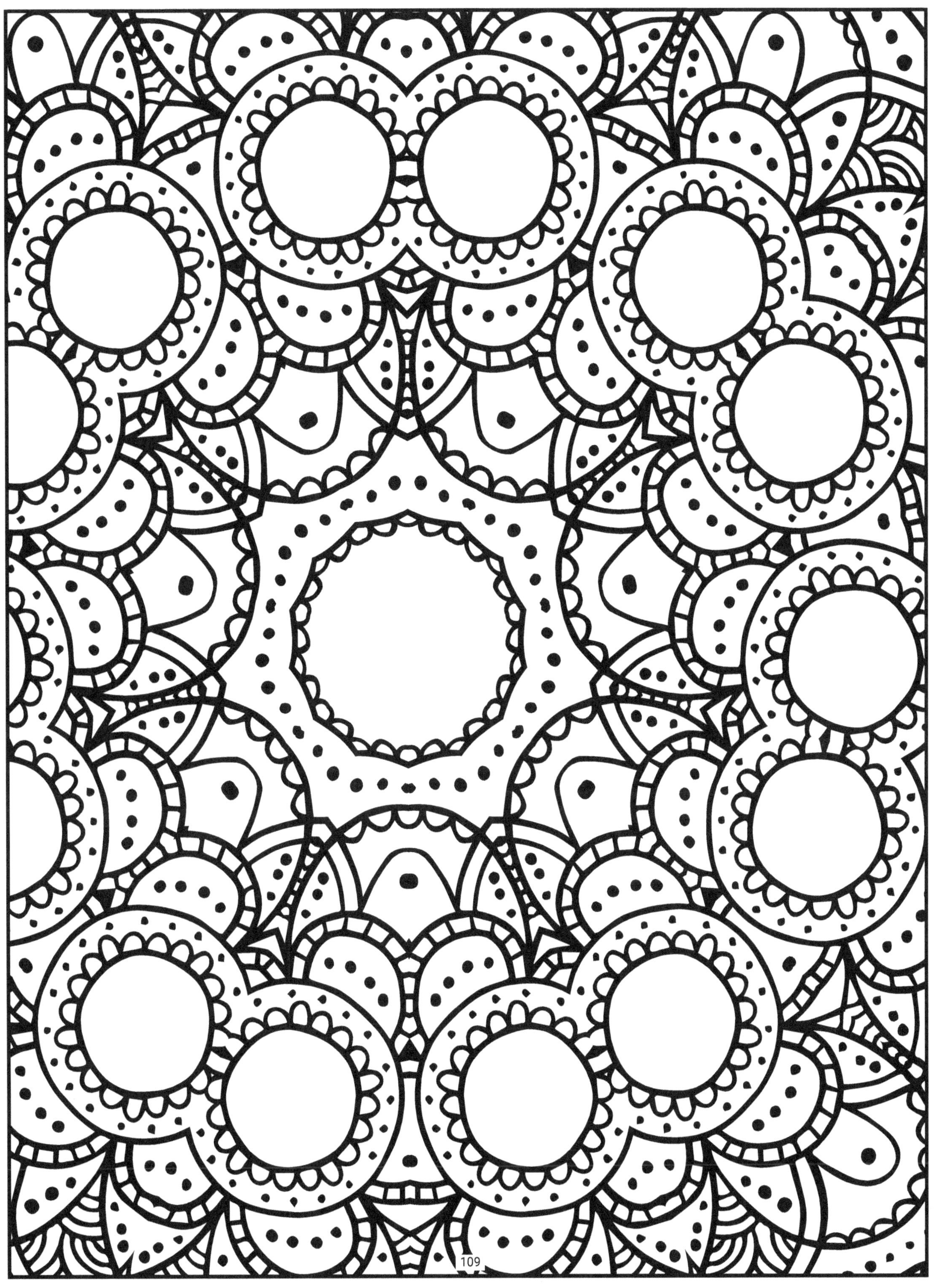

What Emotions Are Emerging as You Color?

What Symbolism or Significance Do You Attribute to the Colors You've Chose?

Can You Describe the Story or Narrative Behind Your Colorful Picture?

What new things come up from the old memories and experiences?

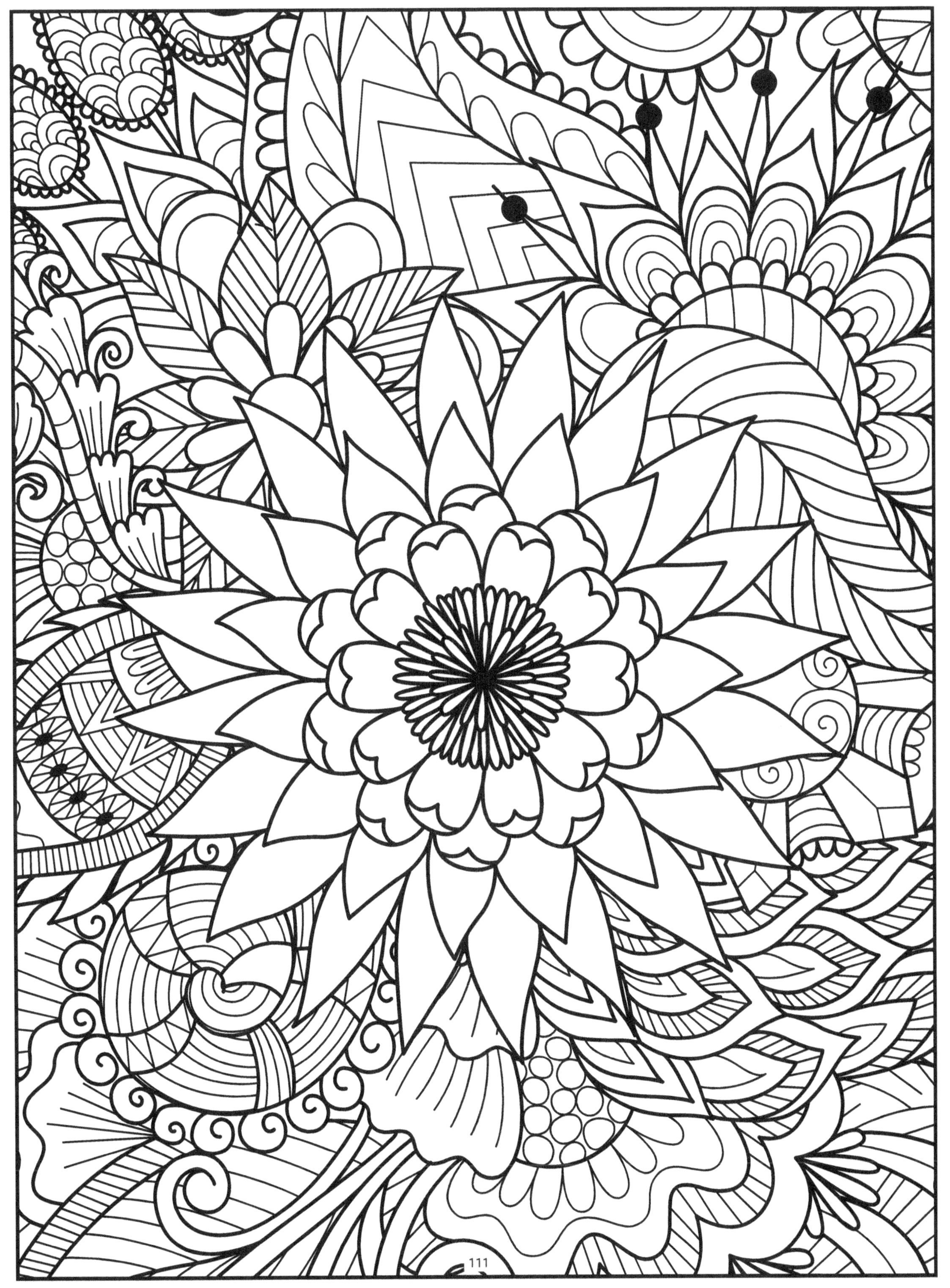

What Emotions Are Emerging as You Color?

What Symbolism or Significance Do You Attribute to the Colors You've Chose?

Can You Describe the Story or Narrative Behind Your Colorful Picture?

What new things come up from the old memories and experiences?

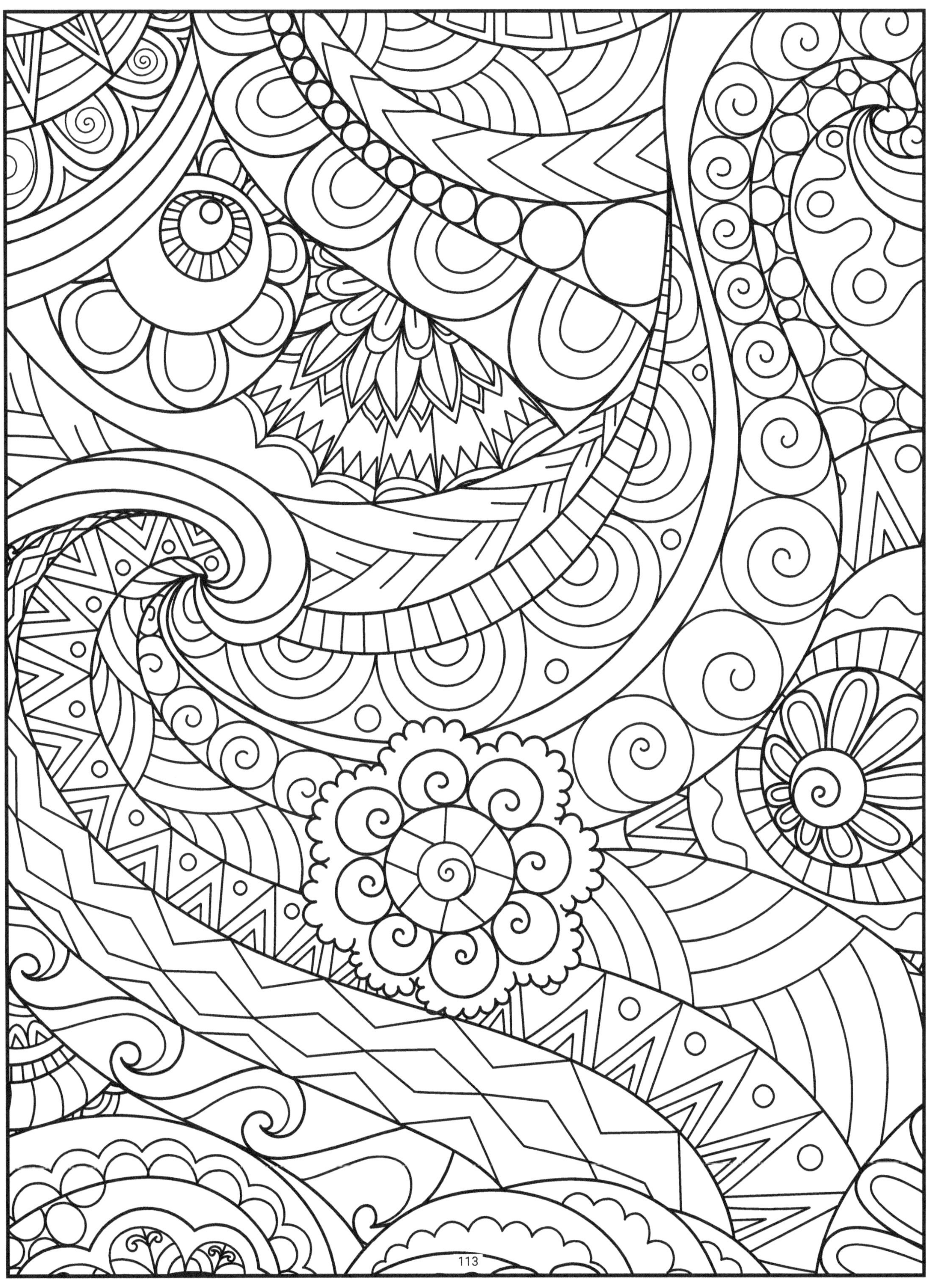

What Emotions Are Emerging as You Color?

What Symbolism or Significance Do You Attribute to the Colors You've Chose?

Can You Describe the Story or Narrative Behind Your Colorful Picture?

What new things come up from the old memories and experiences?

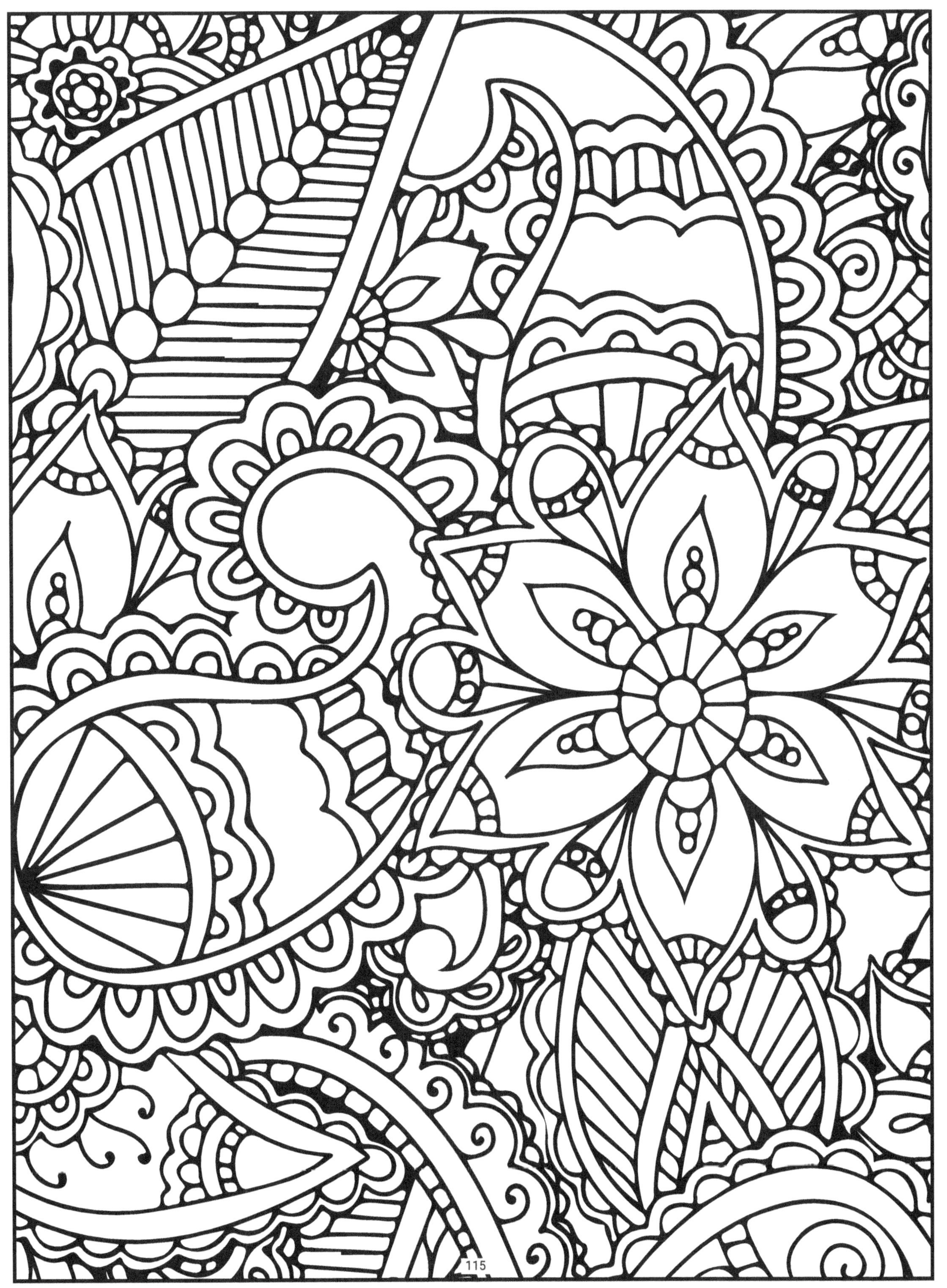

What Emotions Are Emerging as You Color?

What Symbolism or Significance Do You Attribute to the Colors You've Chose?

Can You Describe the Story or Narrative Behind Your Colorful Picture?

What new things come up from the old memories and experiences?

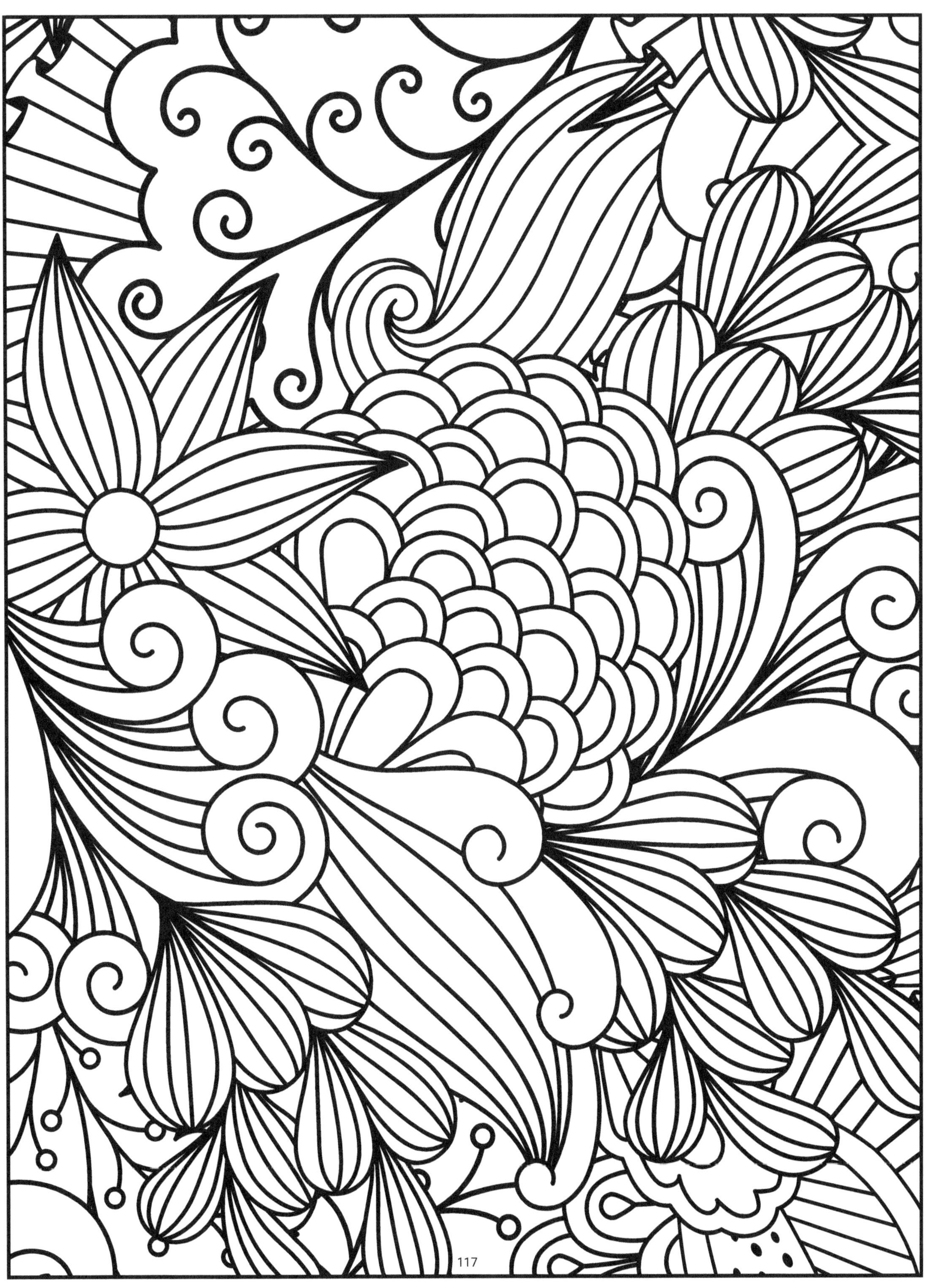

What Emotions Are Emerging as You Color?

What Symbolism or Significance Do You Attribute to the Colors You've Chose?

Can You Describe the Story or Narrative Behind Your Colorful Picture?

What new things come up from the old memories and experiences?

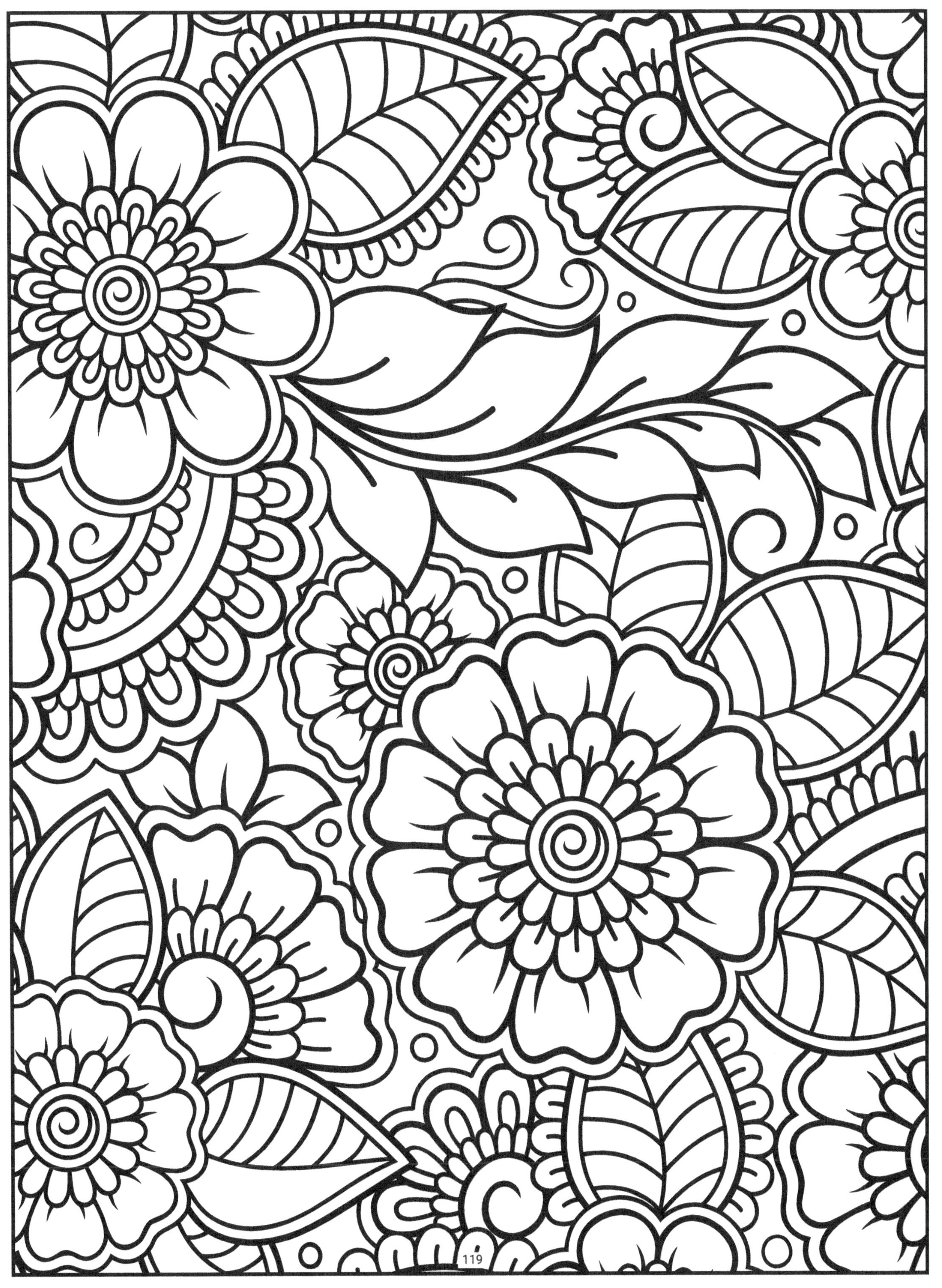

What Emotions Are Emerging as You Color?

What Symbolism or Significance Do You Attribute to the Colors You've Chose?

Can You Describe the Story or Narrative Behind Your Colorful Picture?

What new things come up from the old memories and experiences?

What Emotions Are Emerging as You Color?

What Symbolism or Significance Do You Attribute to the Colors You've Chose?

Can You Describe the Story or Narrative Behind Your Colorful Picture?

What new things come up from the old memories and experiences?

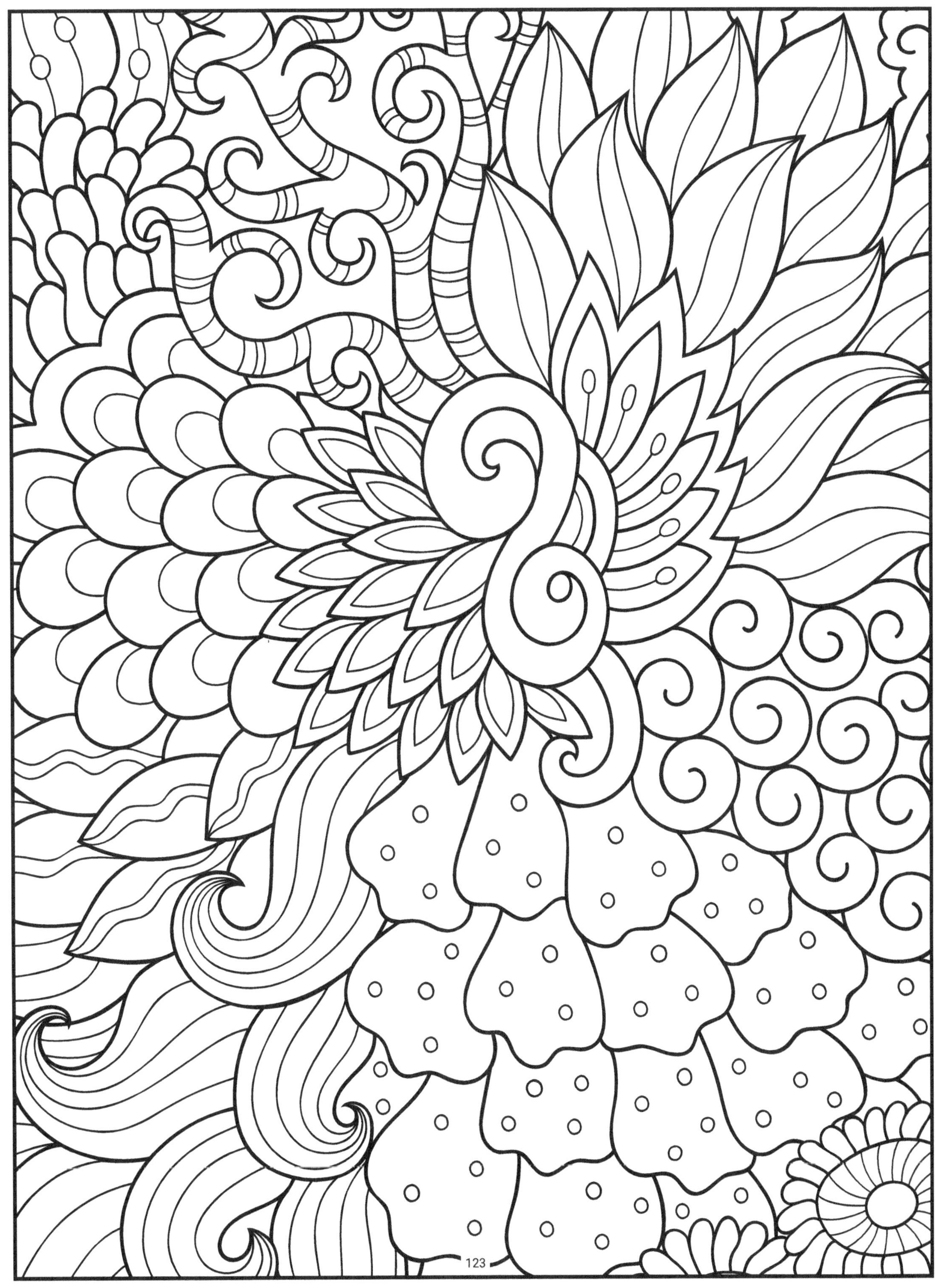

What Emotions Are Emerging as You Color?

What Symbolism or Significance Do You Attribute to the Colors You've Chose?

Can You Describe the Story or Narrative Behind Your Colorful Picture?

What new things come up from the old memories and experiences?